The BIG Book of QUESTIONS and ANSWERS

ARCTURUS

ARCTURUS

This edition published in 2021 by Arcturus Publishing Limited
26/27 Bickels Yard, 151–153 Bermondsey Street,
London SE1 3HA

Authors: Claire Philip and Polly Cheeseman
Illustrator: Jean Claude
Editors: Violet Peto and Becca Clunes
Designer: Trudi Webb, Stefan Holliland and Sally Bond
Editorial Manager: Joe Harris

ISBN: 978-1-3988-1103-4
CH010031NT
Supplier 29, Date 1021, Print run 11734

Printed in China

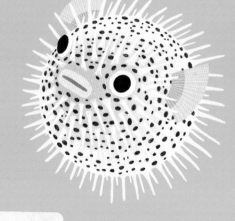

CONTENTS

Are You a Curious Kid?........4

Jungle Animals.................5

Woodland Creatures.........47

Our World....................89

The Ocean...................125

Space 167

How Things Work 209

Glossary 251

Index 254

Answers 256

ARE YOU A CURIOUS KID?

Do you love to ask questions and find out about the world?
This book is filled with all kinds of information on different topics.
Here are some of the questions that you can find the answers to.

Why do we have
day and night?

What do
astronauts eat?

How do beavers
build their dams?

How do
clocks tell
the time?

Which sea creature
has a head the
shape of a hammer?

Why do chameleons
have long tongues?

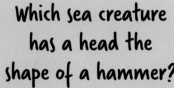

JUNGLE ANIMALS

JUNGLE HOMES

Many animals make their homes in the jungle.

HARPY EAGLE

Where do jaguars sleep?

They climb trees and find a comfortable branch to sleep on.

Which jungle insect builds tall towers?

Termites do! They make them from soil.

Where do monkeys find food?

In the treetops! They find lots of
different fruits to eat there.

Do parrots build nests?

No, they nest in holes in tree trunks.
Other birds, such as harpy eagles,
build nests from twigs and leaves.

Can tapirs climb trees?

No, they can't! They live on the forest
floor and sometimes hide among bushes.

Where do tree frogs rest?

They rest on leaves to keep
them nice and damp.

ON THE FOREST FLOOR

On the dark, damp rain forest floor,
very few green plants grow.

How do wild pigs find food?

They use their snouts to snuffle along
the ground and find tasty roots to eat.

Which animal eats brazil nuts?

Agoutis! These creatures search
for fallen brazil nuts to
crunch open.

Where do giant centipedes hide?

Along with many other jungle insects,
they hide among rotting leaves.

**How do ocelots
hunt for food?**
They use their excellent
eyesight to help them see
in the low light.

How do snakes protect their eggs?
Snakes that lay their eggs on the ground
coil up on top of them to protect
the babies growing inside.

**Do spiders live on
the forest floor?**
Some big tarantulas do!

**How do toads hide
from predators?**
Their green skin blends into
their surroundings.

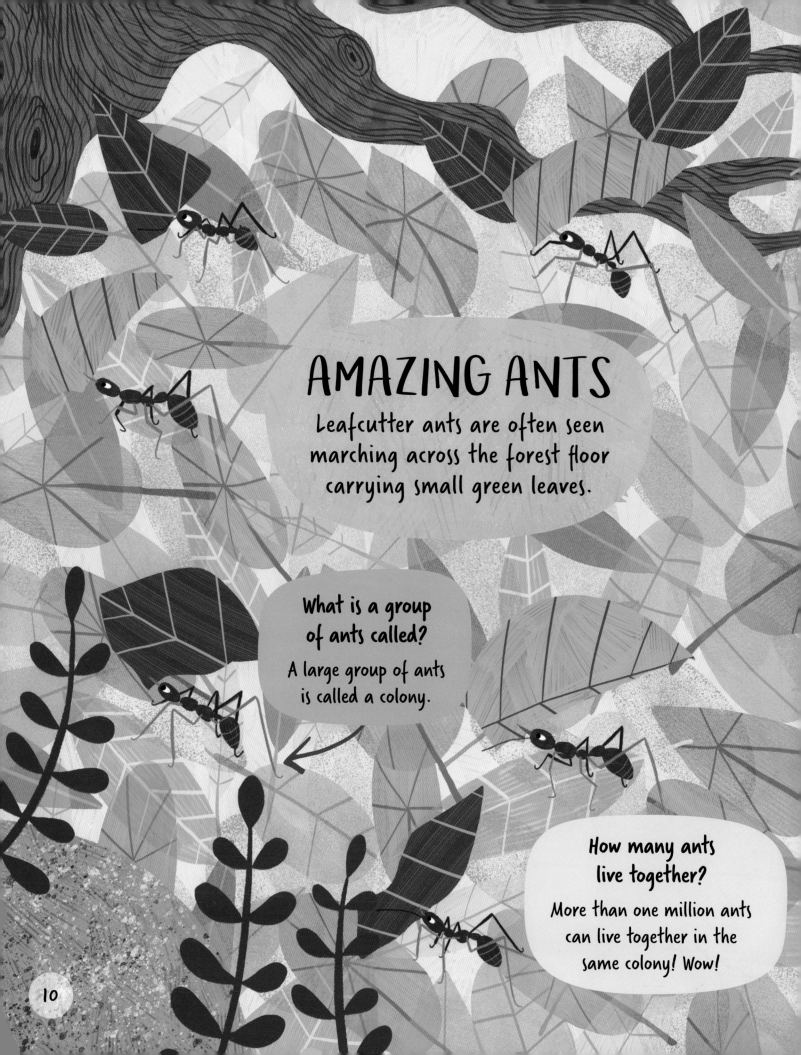

AMAZING ANTS

Leafcutter ants are often seen marching across the forest floor carrying small green leaves.

What is a group of ants called?

A large group of ants is called a colony.

How many ants live together?

More than one million ants can live together in the same colony! Wow!

Where do the ants take the leaves?
Back to their nest. They are placed in a special area where they grow a fungus that feeds the colony.

What eats leafcutter ants?
Leafcutter ants are food for many jungle creatures including giant anteaters.

How do anteaters eat ants?
Anteaters slurp up ants using their long tongues.

11

TERRIFIC TIGERS

Bengal tigers hide in the grasses of Asian rain forests.

Why do tigers have stripes?

Their patterns make them hard to spot, so they can easily sneak up on prey.

Are tigers identical?

No. Amazingly, no two tigers have the same pattern of stripes!

How loud is a tiger's roar?

Very loud! It can be heard a few miles away!

How do tiger cubs stay safe?

Cubs have even more stripes than adults to give them better camouflage.

When do tigers hunt for prey?

Tigers usually attack at night. They will travel long distances to find animals to eat.

Which animals do tigers attack?

They hunt many animals such as monkeys, birds, and even elephants!

Why do tiger cubs playfight?

They fight to prepare for attacking real prey.

Do tiger cubs stay with their mothers?

No. When they are ready, they leave to find their own areas to hunt.

13

GREAT GORILLAS

Gorillas are some of the most powerful yet gentle animals of the rain forest. They are closely related to you and me!

What do gorillas do all day?

In the morning, jungle gorillas sit and eat. In the afternoon, they sleep, play, and groom each other.

What do they eat?

They mostly eat plants, fruit, tree bark, and insects.

Where do gorillas sleep?

At night, gorillas sleep in their snug nests, which they build from leaves and sticks.

14

Are gorillas a type of monkey?

No—they are a type of animal called an ape.

What is a silverback?

The male leader of a family group of gorillas.

15

ON THE RIVERBANK

On a rain forest riverbank, many animals come together to sunbathe, drink, hunt, or play.

Where do dwarf caiman live?

Dwarf caiman are members of the alligator family. They build burrows to rest in before going out to hunt.

RIVER OTTERS

Do turtles swim in rivers?

Yes! Amazon River turtles swim along the riverbank and lay their eggs in sunny spots.

What are capybaras?

Capybaras are animals that look like large guinea pigs. They spend most of their time grazing on plants on the riverbank.

Can snakes swim?

Anacondas can! These snakes move more quickly in the water than on land.

Why are some people scared of piranhas?

These fish swim in a group and have sharp teeth. They don't attack humans, though.

Do manatees live alone?
No, they live in small groups.

What do manatees eat?
They nibble on underwater plants. When food is hard to find, they live off their body fat.

18

MAGICAL MANATEES

Amazonian manatees, or sea cows, swim in freshwater lagoons in the rain forest.

Are mantaees speedy swimmers?

No, they aren't! These calm animals are very shy and secretive, and they move very slowly.

Can dolphins be pink?

One kind can—the pink river dolphin. Sadly, these large, beautiful dolphins are very rare today. If you spot one, you are lucky.

19

DEADLY JAGUARS

Jaguars are the third-biggest cats in the world, after lions and tigers.

Do jaguars live in groups?

No, jaguars prefer to live alone. They leave claw marks on trees to mark their areas.

Do jaguars eat large prey?

Yes, they do! They hunt animals as large as this caiman.

How big do caimans grow?

They can grow as long as a giraffe is tall!

Are jaguars stripey?
No, they have black, rose-shaped spots.

Can jaguars swim?
Yes, they are very good swimmers. They will sometimes swim through rivers to get to their prey.

When do jaguars hunt?
At night—when caimans come out to search for food!

21

IN THE UNDERSTORY

The understory is an area above the forest floor, where the bushes and grasses grow.

Do lots of animals live in this layer?

Yes! Many animals, such as this Amazon salamander, live in the trees and bushes.

Do bats live in rain forests?

They do. Greater bulldog bats can be found flying through the understory on their way to lagoons.

Which insect looks like a leaf?
This praying mantis! It can blend in with the leaves perfectly.

How do treefrogs catch bugs?
By sitting on plants and flicking out their long, sticky tongues!

How big are hercules beetles?
About the size of an adult's hand! Amazingly, these heavy beetles can fly.

POISONOUS FROGS

Poison dart frogs are easy to spot. They can be red, yellow, green, blue, and black!

How big is a poison dart frog?

Tiny. They are about as big as an adult's thumbnail.

Why do they have bright patterns?

To warn other animals that they are dangerous to eat.

Do they come from tadpoles?

Yes, just like other frogs, poison dart frogs lay eggs that hatch into tadpoles.

Are they dangerous?

Yes, very. The golden poison dart frog is the most poisonous. Touching one would make a human very sick!

Do poison dart frogs live in ponds?

No, they live in small pools of rainwater that collect inside trees and plants.

How do they get to the pools?

Once the eggs hatch, the frog parents take the tadpoles to pools of water by carrying them on their backs!

25

SCALY CHAMELEONS

In the forests of Madagascar, off the coast of Africa, lives the panther chameleon.

Can a chameleon change the shade of its skin?

Yes! A chameleon's skin can change depending on its mood.

Can chameleons climb?

Yes—they have special feet that allow them to grip onto the branches.

What do they eat?
Birds, other small lizards, and lots of bugs, such as this moth!

How long is a chameleon's tongue?
Their tongues can be longer than their bodies! They are sticky to help them catch prey.

Why are a chameleon's eyes unusual?
Because they can move separately, giving them excellent eyesight.

Do snakes climb trees?

Yes! Emerald tree boas curl
up on thick jungle branches to rest
and wait for prey.

**Why are some emerald
tree boas red?**

Young boas have red bodies
with white zigzags—the
adults have green bodies.

SLITHERING SNAKES

Rain forest snakes often have green bodies to help them blend in with the leaves. This makes it hard for birds of prey to catch them.

How do boas attack their prey?

First, a boa bites. Then it squeezes the prey until it stops moving.

Do snakes have special senses?

Yes! They can sense the body heat from nearby prey, such as mice.

How often does a snake eat?

Once the prey has been swallowed, the snake is full for weeks or even months!

What grows in the canopy?

Lots of fruit! This makes it a great place for animals to find food.

Why do toucans have long beaks?

To help them pick and peel fruit to eat.

Why do monkeys have strong tails?

To help them hang from the branches as they travel and play!

Can ants build nests off the ground?

Yes! Weaver ants make nests in the canopy using special silk to glue leaves together.

Why don't Saki monkeys leave the trees?

Because their food is found high up off the ground!

IN THE CANOPY

High up in the trees, above the understory is the leafy canopy. It's the busiest place in the jungle!

What do hummingbirds eat?

These tiny birds eat sweet nectar from canopy flowers.

EYELASH VIPER

HOWLER MONKEYS

These large, bearded monkeys live in noisy groups called troops.

Why do howler monkeys howl? To warn other monkeys to stay away! Their calls can be heard for miles.

Are some howler monkeys red?

Yes! Howler monkeys can have black, brown, or red fur.

How do they make so much noise?

The males have extra-large throats to help them make their loud sounds.

What do they eat?

Howler monkeys love to eat leaves, fruits, flowers, and nuts. They have an excellent sense of smell, which they use to track down food.

BIRDS OF PARADISE

Birds of paradise are some of the most amazing rain forest birds of all.

How did birds of paradise get their name?

Years ago, people thought that these birds came from the heavens, or "paradise."

Do males and females look the same?

No. The female has dull, brown feathers since she doesn't need to impress a male.

Who looks after the chicks?

The female birds of paradise.

Why are the males so fancy?
The males have bright, fancy feathers
to attract females.

Do they dance?
Almost! This male Raggiana bird-of-paradise claps his
wings and shakes his head to impress a female.

SLOW-MOVING SLOTHS

Sloths are sleepy, tree-dwelling creatures that rarely come down to the ground.

Why do moths like sloths?

Moths and other insects make their homes on sloths. Amazing!

Why do sloths move slowly?

To save as much energy as possible!

Do sloths ever touch the ground?

Yes, but rarely. They only visit the forest floor once a week to poop!

Why do sloths have long claws?
They need them to grip firmly onto branches as they rest!

Do sloths have predators?
Yes. Eagles and big cats hunt sloths.

37

AWESOME ORANGUTANS

Orangutans are known for their orange hair.
They live high up in the tallest trees, yet they do
sometimes visit the forest floor.

Where do orangutans sleep?

They sleep in snug nests, which
they make from branches
and leaves.

**Do baby
orangutans
need lots of care?**

Yes they do—they stay
with their mothers until
they are a few years old.

Are they in danger?

Very sadly, yes. Many of the forests in which they live are being cut down.

Why do orangutans have such long arms?

An orangutan's arms are long and strong to help them swing from branch to branch!

Do they live in groups?

No. They mostly live alone, unless they are taking care of their young.

Do orangutans have predators?

Yes—leopards and other big cats will hunt them.

39

LIFE AT THE TOP

The very top of the rain forest is called the emergent layer.

Do monkeys love to leap and play?

Yes they do! Squirrel monkeys hop across the treetops like acrobats!

What is a group of monkeys called?

Monkeys travel in groups called troops. Together they search for shoots, buds, and leaves to eat.

Can parrots reach the treetops?

Yes. Scarlet macaws are large parrots that can be seen in the emergent layer.

What are the tallest jungle plants?

Brazil nut trees and kapok trees are the tallest plants in the rain forest.

Can bats fly up high?

Yes! Vampire bats often hunt on the ground, but they can be found this high up, too.

Is there lots of food for monkeys at the top of the forest?

Yes, lots! Monkeys, such as capuchins, collect nuts and fruit from up high.

41

BRILLIANT BUTTERFLIES

The blue morpho butterfly is one of the largest and most beautiful insects in the rain forest.

Do blue morphos gather in big groups?

Yes! Pilots flying planes over the jungle often spot large groups of these butterflies from above.

Why do blue morphos have brown underwings?

To protect them as they rest. Predators are less likely to spot dull shades.

42

How big is a blue morpho?
From wing to wing, they are the length of a banana!

How do they taste their food?
The butterflies taste with their feet! They smell the air with their antennae.

Do they only fly at the top of the forest?
No—groups of these butterflies flutter throughout the layers of the forest.

43

FIERCE EAGLES

Few other jungle birds fly as high as the fierce harpy eagle.

How high can harpy eagles fly? This amazing hunter can fly to the top of the tallest rain forest trees!

What do harpy eagles eat? They will catch and eat smaller birds, iguanas, monkeys—and even sloths!

44

Do any animals hunt harpy eagles?
No—they are too difficult to catch!

How big are their claws?
Very large! The eagles use their enormous claws, or talons, to grip onto prey.

How often do harpy eagles have chicks?
A mating pair will usually raise a chick every few years. They hunt meat for their baby for around 12 months.

Can they fly very fast?
Yes! Even though the female is almost twice the size of the male, it is super speedy.

45

JUNGLE ANIMALS QUIZ

How well do you remember facts about jungle animals?
Decide if these sentences are true or false, then check
your answers on page 256.

1 Orangutans have brown fur and long tails.

2 Male birds of paradise show off their feathers to attract a female.

3 A group of monkeys is called a school.

4 Jaguars sleep in burrows they dig themselves.

5 Chameleons have long, sticky tongues.

6 A silverback is a male gorilla.

7 Tapirs climb trees to find fruit to eat.

8 You are safe from snakes if you stand in a river.

WOODLAND CREATURES

WHAT IS A WOODLAND?

Woodlands and forests are places that are covered in trees. Most woodlands are made up of lots of different species (types) of trees and plants.

Which trees stay green all year?

Coniferous trees— they do not lose their leaves at all!

Which trees change from season to season?

Deciduous trees— they lose their leaves in the winter and grow new ones in spring.

Do lots of animals live in woodlands?

Yes! All kinds of animals from woodpeckers and badgers to snakes and butterflies make woodlands their home.

Why do animals love trees?

The trees give the animals excellent shelter and provide them with plenty of food.

What happens to fallen leaves in deciduous forests?

Wriggling worms on the woodland floor eat them up!

49

EVERGREEN FORESTS

Coniferous forests stay green all year round. They are found in places that have long winters and lots of rain.

Do conifers grow on mountains?

Trees are not usually found at the top of mountains, but there are often conifer forests farther down.

What kinds of birds live in these forests?

Small birds such as chickadees and large birds such as hawks!

Hawk

Do bears live in coniferous woods?
Yes, they do—along with other large animals, such as lynx, caribou, and wolves.

Which tree species are coniferous?
Trees such as pines, firs, and larches. They keep their leaves all year.

51

CHANGING SEASONS

In a deciduous forest, the trees lose their leaves when the months get colder. Deciduous forests look very different with each season.

What do deciduous woods look like in winter?

Very bare! In winter, deciduous trees have no leaves, and there is little life on the ground.

When do trees grow new leaves?

In the spring! Longer days and more daylight spur new growth.

What happens in the summer?

In the summer, the woodland flourishes. Wildflowers, berries, and fruit grow at this time.

Why do trees lose their leaves?

Before winter, trees lose their leaves to help them save energy over the cold winter months.

Which animals live in these woods?

Deciduous woods make perfect homes for deer, weasels, rabbits, robins, frogs, and more!

53

AMONG THE LEAF LITTER

The forest floor is covered with dead wood and fallen leaves called leaf litter.

Who keeps the forest tidy?

Worms and snails! They help clean up the forest floor by eating up the rotting plant life.

Where does fungi grow?

All over fallen trees. Fungi makes a special juice that breaks down dead wood.

Which animals live on the forest floor?

All kinds of insects and worms. There is plenty for them to eat here.

Do frogs live in the woods?

They do! The forest floor is cool and damp enough for them to survive here.

Where do adders like to lurk?

Among the leaf litter!

THE AMAZING UNDERGROWTH

The shady bottom layer
of a woodland is called
the undergrowth.

What do wild boar eat?
They eat beechnuts that
fall from beech trees.

56

Do rabbits play in the undergrowth?

Yes! Rabbits—and hares—are found in this part of the woods.

When are badgers most active?

Badgers roam around at dusk and dawn. They mostly eat earthworms.

What animals can be seen on leaves?

Caterpillars crawl over leaves as they munch on them!

UP HIGH

Animals such as squirrels, bats, and many birds make their homes high up in the trees.

What do baby blackbirds eat?

Blackbird chicks love to eat wriggly worms. Cheep cheep!

Where do owls sleep?

Owls sleep in nooks in the trees during the day. They mostly come out to hunt at night.

Do squirrels share their nests?

Sometimes! If it is very cold, squirrels will cozy up with each other in their nests called dreys.

Do woodpeckers build nests?

No, they simply find a hole in a tree high off the ground. Woodpeckers take turns fetching food for their chicks.

59

FOLLOW THE TRACKS

If you look closely at mud on the forest floor,
you can find footprints left behind by
many different animals.

What do deer prints look like?
Deer hooves leave two
long marks, usually with
a point at the front.

**Which animal leaves tracks
that look like arrowheads?**
Birds such as pheasants!

What do fox tracks look like?
Fox tracks show four toes in a kind of diamond shape.

Which bird drops acorns as it flies?
Some birds, such as the jay, leave tracks behind in the form of dropped food, such as acorns.

Which creature leaves claw marks?
Badgers leave behind large claw marks that look like a cat's, but bigger.

61

NUTS AND BERRIES

Woodlands are great places for animals to find plenty of nuts, seeds, and berries to eat.

What do deer eat?

Deer wander the forests looking for flowers, berries, bark, and nuts to nibble on.

How do animals sow seeds?

After eating berries, the seeds pass through an animal's body and out in its droppings. The seeds then grow into new plants!

Why do mice hide their food?

Wood mice gather up lots of nuts and hide them in an underground burrow to eat at a later time.

Why do waxwings have big beaks?

Because they eat a lot of fruit! Their beaks can open unusually wide to help them eat large berries.

HUNGRY HUNTERS

Woodlands are home to many animals that hunt for food.

What is a group of wolves called?

A wolf pack. The pack works together as a team to find food.

What do golden eagles hunt?

They hunt animals, such as rabbits, and can spot them from high above the ground.

Why are golden eagles such good hunters?

They have excellent eyesight to help them pinpoint prey.

How do they catch their prey?

Using their sharp claws called talons.

Can a wolf pack catch a moose?

Yes! It might take them a long time, but a wolf pack can bring down an animal as big as a moose or an elk.

IN THE NIGHT

Lots of woodland creatures sleep in the day and come out at night.

When do bats wake up?

Around sunset! They then swoop and dart across the sky as they hunt for insects to eat.

Which insect lays its eggs at night?

In summertime, heart moths lay their eggs on the branches of oak trees after dark.

What do hedgehogs eat?

They eat the worms, slugs, and snails that rustle around in fallen leaves.

What makes owls so quiet?
Thanks to special feathers, owls fly silently though the night. Their prey can't hear them coming!

Are foxes good at hunting?
Yes! Foxes have excellent hearing that helps them find mice in the dark. Then they sneak up and pounce!

Why do barn owls come out at night?
To find small prey, such as mice, to eat—and to feed to their young chicks.

67

WOODLAND DIARY: OCTOBER

As the weather gets cooler, the leaves in a deciduous forest turn golden, red, and brown before they fall to the ground.

What do wasps eat?
Wasps buzz around eating up sweet, sugary fruits.

When do blackberries ripen?
Blackberries on bramble bushes begin to ripen in late summer.

Can hoverflies sting?
No. Hoverflies may look like wasps, but they cannot sting.

Which bird dips and dives in a large group?

Huge groups of starlings come together in the evenings. They fly around in the sky looking for somewhere to rest for the night.

What is a group of starlings called?

A murmuration!

69

WOODLAND DIARY: JANUARY

In wintertime, the weather gets very cold, and deciduous trees have no leaves left. There is very little food for the animals to eat.

Why do squirrels hide their nuts?
So that they have something to eat during the cold winter months!

Why are winter berries red?
To make them easy for birds to find— and eat!

How do wild ponies keep warm?

Like many animals, they grow a special, thick winter coat to keep them warm.

Which woodland creature sleeps through winter?

Hedgehogs escape the cold by hibernating in winter. This means that they go into a special kind of sleep—all winter long!

71

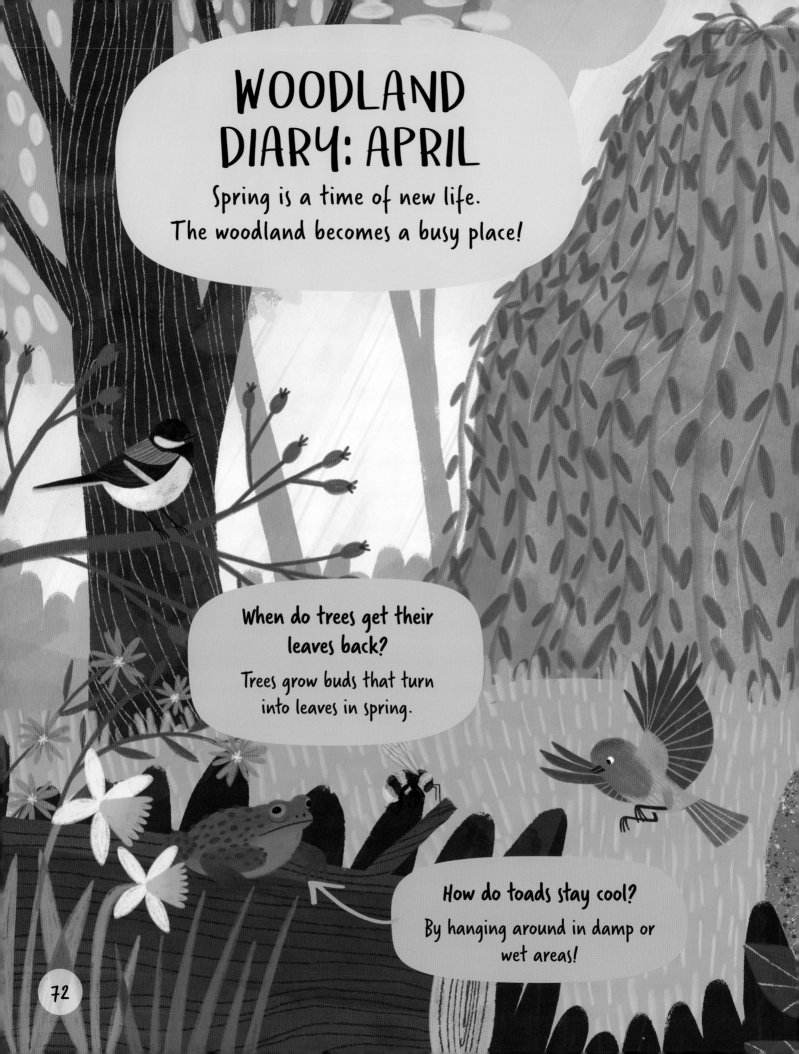

WOODLAND DIARY: APRIL

Spring is a time of new life.
The woodland becomes a busy place!

When do trees get their leaves back?

Trees grow buds that turn into leaves in spring.

How do toads stay cool?

By hanging around in damp or wet areas!

Why do birds sing?

It is how they speak to each other. The woodland in spring is noisy with birdsong.

When do baby birds hatch?

Just like many other animals, they hatch in the spring. Birds' nests are full with eggs and baby chicks at this time.

WOODLAND DIARY: JULY

In warm, sunny summer, leafy trees make lots of shade on the forest floor.

What does a wasp nest look like?

They look like long, papery balloons! You may spot them hanging from tree branches.

Do butterflies live in woods?

Yes, some do. They can be found fluttering from flower to flower.

What do bees eat?

They eat a sweet juice called nectar that comes from inside flowers. Bees collect it and bring it back to their hive to feed to other bees.

Why do spiders spin webs?

They spin sticky webs to catch insects for their dinner!

AN UNDERGROUND WORLD

Below the surface of the woodland floor, there is a lot of activity.

Which animal lives in a warren?

A rabbit. A warren is a network of underground burrows.

Which animals hunt rabbits?

Animals such as foxes hunt rabbits. Rabbits build their homes underground to try and keep away from them.

Which animal lives in a sett?

A badger. A sett is a series of underground tunnels.

Why do badgers have such big claws?

Their long, powerful claws are used for digging.

Does a badger sleep in its sett?

Yes, it does. Badgers also use their setts for storing food, and female badgers have their babies underground.

77

WOODLAND RIVER CREATURES

Lots of different creatures live alongside the rivers that wind through woodlands.

Why do birds visit riverbanks?

Birds, such as common sandpipers and oystercatchers, search for food on the riverbanks.

What do river otters eat?

They eat all kinds of prey, from fish and worms, to birds, eggs, and even frogs.

Are river otters good swimmers?

Yes! They are built for swimming—their smooth bodies help them move through the water easily.

Can they go on land?

Yes—they can live both on land and in water.

79

BUSY AS A BEAVER

Beavers like to live around fresh running water surrounded by woodland.

Why do beavers build dams?
To slow down the flow of the river and make ponds of still water.

Do they live in the dams?
Yes! They build homes called lodges in the ponds to live in and keep safe from predators.

Do beavers have bedrooms?
Yes! Inside the lodges are special rooms for sleeping and for eating.

How do bevers cut down trees?

With their teeth! Large teeth help beavers bite into trees and split them into smaller branches.

What do beavers eat?

They eat plants, bark, twigs, and leaves.

THE SALMON RUN

Every year, salmon go on an incredible journey that often ends in forest rivers.

Where do salmon lay their eggs?

After spending time at sea, millions of salmon swim up rivers. They lay eggs in the very same place they were born!

Which animals hunt salmon?

In the rivers of North America, large grizzly bears gather to hunt the salmon that swim past.

Do birds eat salmon, too?

Yes! Overhead, bald eagles circle, waiting for their chance to dive and catch salmon.

How do bears catch fish?

Bears use their long claws to hook salmon out of the water.

SCALY AND SLITHERING

Some reptiles live in woodlands, but they are shy, so we don't often see them.

Do lizards sunbathe?
Yes! Lizards love to bask in the Sun to soak up its warmth.

Where do snakes lay their eggs?
Some snakes nest in a hole in the ground. Others lay their eggs in warm, rotting leaf litter.

Do snakes have legs?
No—they slither along the leafy forest floor on their smooth bellies.

How do venomous snakes attack?
They bite their prey with their fangs, injecting poison so their victims can't move.

Are slowworms a kind of snake?
They look like snakes, but they are actually legless lizards!

SHOW-OFFS

Many woodland creatures fight and show off to impress each other. This is their way of finding a mate.

What happens during a deer rut?

During a rut (fight), the leading male deer gathers together the females in his herd.

Why do male deers fight?

The younger males challenge the leader to see who is the strongest.

Do they fight with their antlers?

Yes! They toss their heads, crashing their antlers together. Whoever wins the battle is the new leading male.

Why do buzzards fly in circles?
Up in the sky, buzzards dance to attract a mate. They perform a soaring, looping movement through the air.

Why do dragonflies dance?
Emperor dragonflies dance together when they are choosing a mate.

WOODLAND ANIMALS QUIZ

How well do you remember facts about woodland animals? Decide if these sentences are true or false, then check your answers on page 256.

1 Conifer forests lose their leaves in winter.

2 Beavers live in homes called setts.

3 Wolves hunt together in packs.

4 Eagles have sharp claws called talons.

5 Grizzly bears eat salmon.

6 Owls mostly hunt during the day.

7 Wild boar love to eat beechnuts.

8 Toads live in dry places.

OUR WORLD

WHAT IS PLANET EARTH?

Our wonderful home planet is called Earth. It travels around the Sun once each year. Every single day, Earth spins around once. The side facing the Sun has daylight.

THE INTERNATIONAL SPACE STATION

What are satellites?

Around Earth are satellites, such as the International Space Station. These are human-made objects sent into space to gather information.

How old is Earth?

Very old! Experts believe it about 4.5 billion years old.

How much of Earth is covered in water?

Nearly three-quarters of its surface! The rest is covered by land.

How many people live on Earth?

Nearly 8 billion (8,000,000,000)! Wow!

What makes Earth perfect for people?

On our planet, we have food to eat, air to breathe, sunlight to give us light and heat, and water to drink.

INSIDE EARTH

Deep in the middle of Earth is the hard, inner core. It is made of metals called iron and nickel.

How hot is Earth's core?

Very hot! Earth's inner core is nearly as hot as the surface of the Sun!

INNER CORE

OUTER CORE

What makes up the outer core?

The outer core is also made of iron and nickel, but here they are in a soft, melted form.

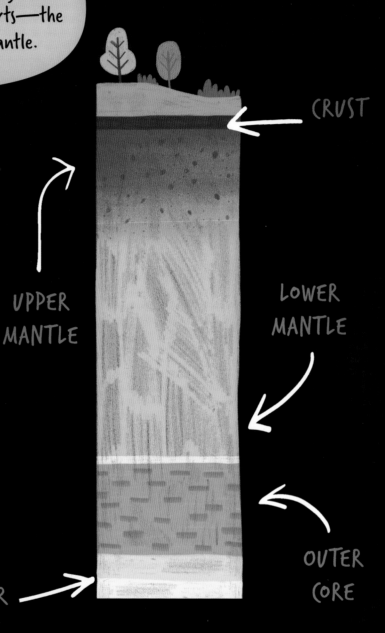

What is above the core?
The next layer up is the mostly solid mantle. It made up of two parts—the upper mantle and lower mantle.

CRUST

UPPER MANTLE

LOWER MANTLE

INNER CORE

OUTER CORE

LOWER MANTLE

UPPER MANTLE

CRUST

Does Earth have a crust?
Yes! The crust is the thinnest layer. It is like a shell around the other layers.

NORTH AMERICA

PACIFIC OCEAN

Where do people live?
Humans live all over the world—in villages, towns, and cities.

WORLD MAP

Earth is made up of seven continents and five major oceans. The continents are called North America, South America, Africa, Europe, Asia, and Oceania.

SOUTH AMERICA

ATLANTIC OCEAN

What's the biggest ocean?
The Pacific! It takes up nearly one third of Earth's surface.

ARCTIC OCEAN

What is the most commonly spoken language?

Mandarin Chinese. People speak different languages all over the world, and lots of people speak more than one language.

EUROPE

ASIA

AFRICA

Do people live in cold areas?

Yes! People live in areas of extreme weather—even in the icy Arctic!

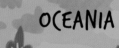

OCEANIA

INDIAN OCEAN

How many animals and plants live on Earth?

Earth is home to millions of plants and animals! They are all perfectly suited to their habitats (homes).

ANTARCTICA

VOLCANOES

When a volcano erupts, hot melted rock bubbles up from deep under ground and bursts out of a mountain as lava.

Do people live near volcanoes?

They do! Land close to volcanoes is often lush, making it excellent for farming.

Are there volcanoes in the sea?

Yes! Volcanoes can also be found under the sea, sometimes forming islands.

Are volcanoes dangerous?

Yes, very. Lava pours over the land, destroying whatever it meets. Hot rocks and ash sometimes shoot out of erupting volcanoes, too!

Do volcanoes stop erupting?

Yes—some volcanoes are extinct, which means that they probably won't ever erupt again.

EARTHQUAKES

In Earth's crust, enormous rocks called tectonic plates move and push against each other, causing earthquakes.

What happens during an earthquake?

The ground on Earth's surface shakes. Take cover!

Are all earthquakes dangerous?

No—some earthquakes are quite small and we can't feel them. Others cause buildings and trees to fall down.

Do earthquakes happen at sea?

Yes, sometimes. They can cause huge waves called tsunamis that are big enough to destroy houses.

Are earthquakes common?

There are some places on Earth where earthquakes happen often, such as the Mid-Atlantic Ridge shown in this picture.

THE WATER CYCLE

Humans, animals, and plants all need water to survive.

RAIN

SNOW

What is the water cycle?

The water cycle is the way water moves around our planet. There are four stages.
1. Water falls from the sky as rain or snow.
2. Some remains as snow or ice. The rest runs into rivers.
3. The rivers flow to the sea.
4. Sea water evaporates and forms rain clouds.

RIVER

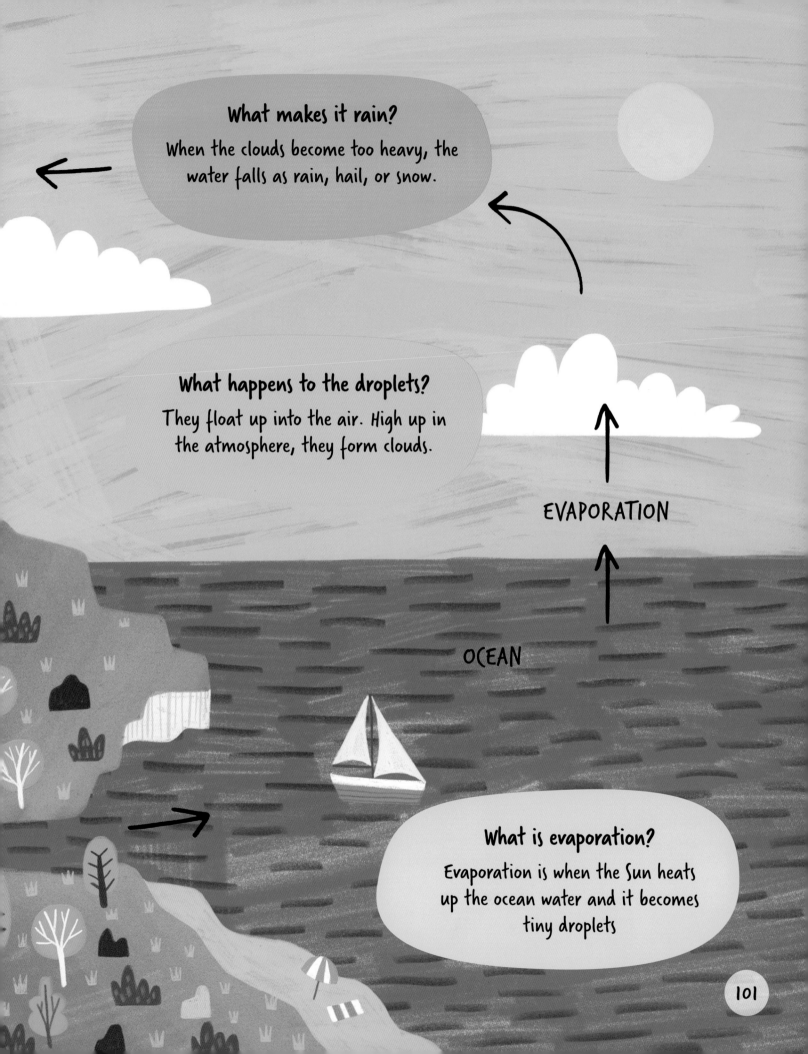

101

RAIN, WIND, AND CLOUDS

Every day when we go outside, we experience the weather.

Can we predict the weather?

Yes! Experts study special weather maps, so they can tell what is coming. They look for features such as the wind and types of clouds.

What do rain clouds look like?

Large, dark clouds often bring lots of rain or even thunderstorms.

Which clouds look like blankets?

Stratus clouds look like thin sheets or blankets. They may mean a fine drizzle is on its way.

What do you call a weather expert?
Somebody who studies the weather is called a meteorologist.

Why does the weather change?
The weather is always changing, depending on what is happening in Earth's atmosphere.

What do wispy clouds mean?
Wispy clouds usually mean mild weather is coming.

WILD WEATHER

Some kinds of weather are wild and even dangerous.

What causes a lightning storm?

A lightning storm happens when small, frozen raindrops bump into each other inside a thundercloud making electricity. This then jumps to the ground with a flash.

What is a hurricane?

A hurricane is a huge tropical storm with seriously strong winds. Hold on tight!

Do storms have eyes?

Not exactly! The "eye" of a storm is its middle, where it is strangely calm.

What are tornadoes?

Tornadoes are very powerful winds that spin around in a circle.

Why does it hail?

Hail is made inside huge clouds during thunderstorms, often on hot days. The balls of ice can cause lots of damage.

MOUNTAINS

Mountains are formed over many millions of years.

What is a volcanic mountain?

After a volcano spews out hot lava, the lava cools and hardens. Over time, many layers build up to form volcanic mountains.

Do mountains have folds?

Not exactly! Some mountains are formed when two of Earth's tectonic plates push up against each other. These are called fold mountains.

What is an avalanche?

Avalanches are large piles of snow that fall quickly down a mountain slope. They are extremely dangerous.

What kinds of animals live in mountain habitats?

Many amazing creatures live there! In some countries you'll find bears, mountain lions, and even golden eagles.

Do people live near mountains?

Yes! Lots of people live very close to mountains. Their natural beauty attracts many visitors, too.

RIVERS

A river is fresh water that mostly flows toward an ocean, sea, or lake.

Where do rivers start?

Rivers begin high up in the hills where there is the most rainfall or snow.

What is a river's source?

The place where a river starts its journey is called its source.

Can water flow uphill?

No, it can't. Water flows downhill and follows the shape of the land until it reaches the ocean.

Where do seabirds live?

Many live at sea, but some, such as seagulls, may live where the river meets the ocean.

Are rivers useful to humans?

Yes! We use rivers for many things, such as taking things from one place to another on boats. Rivers make the nearby land lush and perfect for farming, too.

RAIN FOREST

Rain forests are very special jungle habitats.

Why are rain forests important?

Rain forests are sometimes called the lungs of the planet. They produce oxygen—the air that we breathe.

Does it rain a lot in the jungle?

Yes! The weather here is hot and damp. Rain forests get huge amounts of rainfall each year.

Do people live in the rain forests?
Yes, such as the Huli tribe
of Papua New Guinea.

Why do the Huli tribe collect feathers?
The Huli tribe use feathers to decorate
their headdresses.

DESERTS

Deserts are very dry areas of land with little rain. Some are extremely hot, while some are very cold.

Is there life in the desert?

The lack of water makes it difficult for plants and animals to live in deserts, but many still do.

Do people live there, too?

Yes, people such as the Bedouin tribe often live in deserts. They travel from place to place and don't stay in one location for too long.

Where are deserts found?

Deserts can be found all over the world, from the Sahara in Africa to the Gobi Desert in Asia.

Can deserts be cold?

Yes! Even freezing cold Antarctica is a desert—because there is not much rainfall there at all.

How long can camels go without water?

Camels can go for months without water! They live in deserts easily.

113

NORTH AND SOUTH POLES

The North Pole is at the very top part of Earth.

Is there land at the North Pole?

No—there is no land here, only thick ice and snow.

NORTH POLE

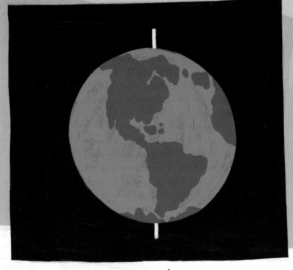

SOUTH POLE

Where is the South Pole?

It is at the very bottom part of Earth, on Antarctica—one of Earth's seven continents.

Where is the Arctic?
Around the North Pole is an area of land known as the Arctic.

Who lives there?
The Inuit people live in the Arctic. They make homes from ice and snow during winter months.

Do people live near the South Pole?
Scientists and explorers visit the South Pole. They study the land and the wildlife.

UNDER THE SEA

Oceans and seas take up much of planet Earth.

Have we explored all of Earth's oceans?

No, not even close! Much of the world's oceans and seas are yet to be explored.

Where does coral grow?

Coral reefs are found close to the edges of islands in warm waters.

Are ocean creatures in danger?
Yes, they are. Due to pollution and overfishing, many sea creatures are under threat.

How can people protect the oceans?
One great way is to avoid plastic as much of this kind of waste ends up in the oceans. If you do need to use it, make sure you recycle.

SEASHORE

Seashores are found where
the land ends and the sea begins.

Are all beaches sandy?

No—seashores can be rocky and
covered in pebbles as well as sandy.

What are tides?

This is the way water levels
change on a beach. At high
tide, the water is close to the
shore. At low tide, the water
is farther away.

How do sea arches form?

At some seashores, there are rocky cliffs. Over time, the waves can wear away the rock to form arches.

Where do rock pools form?

When the tide comes in, seawater fills up small pools called rock pools. These are great places to spot seashore life.

Which creatures live on the shore?

Starfish, mussels, and crabs can be found living here.

TOWNS AND CITIES

All over the world, people live close together in towns and cities.

Why do cities have so many buildings?

Because all the people need homes, shops, schools, hospitals, and offices.

Why are city buildings so tall?
So they take up less space!

What do people do for fun?
They go to places like museums, restaurants, and parks.

Why is Tokyo famous?
Tokyo in Japan, shown here, is a very busy city. It is known for its bright lights and amazing technology.

What problems do cities face?
Large towns and cities often have problems with car fumes and waste.

THE FUTURE OF THE PLANET

Nature on planet Earth gives us the food,
air, and water we need to live, so we must look
after Earth in return.

Why are insects so important?

Bees, butterflies, and other insects help flowers make seeds
that will grow into new flowers.

Why do we need plants?

We need them because they give
us food, and they make
the air that we breathe.

Can kids make a difference?
Yes! We can all do our best to look after our planet by keeping natural places clean and tidy.

How does recycling help?
Recycling waste, such as paper and plastic, whenever possible helps protect our wildlife. Some waste can be harmful to plants and animals.

OUR WORLD QUIZ

How well do you remember facts about our world?
Decide if these sentences are true or false, then check
your answers on page 256.

1 Deserts are always hot.

2 The Moon travels around Earth.

3 It is very cold in Earth's inner core.

4 The seas and oceans cover less than half of the planet.

5 The most common language is Mandarin Chinese.

6 A volcano that is extinct will definitely erupt again.

7 Evaporation happens when the sun heats up water.

8 Mountains are formed very quickly, in just a few minutes.

THE OCEAN

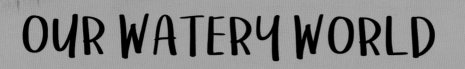

OUR WATERY WORLD

More than two-thirds of our planet is covered with water. The world's oceans are home to millions of plants and animals.

What is an ocean?

An ocean is a very large area of salty water.

What are coasts?

Coasts are places where land meets the sea. Lots of plants and animals live there.

What causes tides?

The Moon's gravity pulls water toward it. This causes the sea to rise and fall along the shore twice every day.

Does ocean water move?

Yes! It flows around Earth in patterns called currents.

Which is the coldest ocean?

The Arctic and the Southern oceans are the coldest, while the Indian Ocean is the warmest.

The Five Oceans of the World

Arctic Ocean

Atlantic Ocean

Pacific Ocean

Indian Ocean

Southern Ocean

127

IN A ROCK POOL

When the tide goes out, small pools of water collect between the rocks on the shore.

Why are rock pools warmer than the rest of the sea?

The water inside a rock pool is shallow, which means the Sun can heat it up more quickly than the rest of the ocean water.

Why do crabs have shells?

Crabs have hard shells to protect them from crashing waves and predators.

How do anemones hunt?

Anemones wave their tentacles in the water, catching food that drifts by.

How do starfish walk?

Starfish have lots of tiny feet on the underside of their arms. They use them to walk on the seabed.

What is seaweed?

Seaweed, such as bladderwrack, is a marine plant. It attaches to rocks and often grows in long strands.

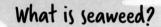

Do shrimp live in rock pools?

Yes, they do! They can be hard to spot as their bodies blend in with their surroundings.

Can limpets move?

Limpets stick their shells firmly onto dry rock, but they can move around under water.

AWESOME OTTERS

Sea otters are mammals. They live along
the coasts of North America and Asia.

Why do otters hold hands?

Sea otters live in groups,
sometimes holding hands so they
don't drift apart as they sleep!

Where does a baby otter sleep?

A sea otter pup (baby) lies on its
mother's tummy as she floats on
her back at the surface.

**How are otters adapted
to life in the water?**

Their thick fur keeps
them warm and dry, and
their webbed feet help
them swim.

How does an otter open a clam shell?

A sea otter puts a rock on its chest and bashes a clam against it. When the shell breaks, the otter eats the insides!

Why do otters dive?

To hunt for sea creatures, such as crabs and clams to eat. Tasty!

Why do otters wrap themselves in seaweed?

As well as holding hands, otters wrap themselves in kelp (a type of seaweed), so they don't float away while they rest.

AMAZING PELICANS

Pelicans are famous for their huge beak pouches,
which they use to scoop up fish from the ocean.

What is a pelican's throat pouch called?

It is called a gular. It can hold three times more water than its stomach can!

How do pelicans catch fish?

When brown pelicans hunt, they fly over the water's surface, then dive headfirst into the waves scooping up fish.

How big are pelicans?
Very large! A pelican's wingspan measures more than the height of a grown person.

Do pelicans drink the water they scoop up?
No. A pelican's special beak drains out the water like a sieve, leaving just the fish behind.

How do pelicans keep their eggs warm?
By standing on them with their large, webbed feet!

SUPER SHARKS

These ancient fish have existed for around 300 million years. Sharks live in every ocean on Earth.

How many species (types) of shark are there?

A lot! Experts believe there are about 300 different shark species.

Do sharks have hundreds of teeth?
Yes! Their teeth are arranged in rows so when a tooth falls out, another moves forward to take its place.

Which shark has a head the shape of a hammer?

You guessed it! The hammerhead shark has a wide, flattened head, which makes it look like a hammer.

Can sharks detect electric currents?

They can! Sea creatures give off tiny electric currents as they move. Sharks can sense these currents, which helps them find food and avoid predators.

How big are tiger sharks?

Watch out! These huge sharks are longer than a family car.

What do tiger sharks eat?

They will eat almost any other creature they can catch! This includes seals, fish, turtles, birds, and even other sharks.

A CORAL REEF

Many creatures make their home in the warm waters of a coral reef.
The largest coral reef is the Great Barrier Reef in Australia.

Which coral reef fish is longer than a person?

The humphead wrasse fish! These giants eat sea urchins, fish, and coral.

How many species of coral are there?

There are thousands of different kinds of coral.

Sea fan

Brain coral

Is coral alive?
Yes! Each coral is a group of tiny creatures called polyps. The polyps make hard layers that form reefs over many years.

Are there snakes in the sea?
Yes! They are called sea snakes. They come to the surface to breathe air and attack prey with a venomous bite.

Table coral

Where do clownfish hide?
Clownfish hide among the tentacles of sea anemones. Unlike other coral reef creatures, they do not feel the anemone's stings.

Why are sea slugs so bright?
Sea slugs have bright, bold patterns to warn predators that they are poisonous to eat.

Giant clam

PECULIAR PORCUPINE FISH

Some ocean creatures have unusual ways to protect themselves from enemies.

How do porcupine fish stay safe from predators?

They make themselves much larger by puffing up like a spiky balloon!

How big do they get?

Porcupine fish can expand to two or three times their normal size.

Puffed up

Are porcupine fish poisonous?

Yes—they are deadly to eat. If their spikes don't harm the animals that hunt them, their poison will.

138

How many different species are there?

There are around 90 different species (types) of porcupine fish.

Normal sized

Where do porcupine fish live?

Porcupine fish are found in warm and shallow waters in the Indian, Pacific, and Atlantic oceans.

CLEVER OCTOPUSES

These curious creatures have some very useful tricks.

How many tentacles do octopuses have?

Each octopus has eight tentacles and each one is covered in suckers. They help octopuses catch hold of crabs and lobsters to eat.

Are octopuses smart?

Yes! They have large donut-shaped brains as well as a minibrain in each of their eight arms.

How do divers find octopuses?

They look in small underwater crevices, holes in rocks, and inside old shells.

Why do octopuses squirt ink?
To hide from their attackers! The ink confuses predators so they leave the octopuses alone.

How do octopuses hide from predators?
To fool predators, mimic octopuses change their body shape. They pretend to be other creatures, such as venomous sea snakes.

141

MAGICAL SEAHORSES

These strange and beautiful fish live
in shallow waters and coral reefs.

**What kind of creature
is a seahorse?**

Seahorses are fish. Instead of scales,
they have bony plates on the outside
of their bodies.

What is the smallest seahorse?

The pygmy seahorse is the smallest!
It is tiny enough to fit on
your fingernail.

What do seahorses eat?

They eat small sea creatures and algae by sucking water through their long snouts.

Do they eat a lot?

Yes, they do! They have to eat nearly all the time as they do not have a stomach. Food passes quickly through their bodies.

Why do seahorses wrap their tails around plants?

To make sure they don't drift away as they rest or feed.

143

GENTLE DUGONGS

These shy mammals spend most of their time on the seabed munching on seagrass.

Where do dugongs live?

Dugongs live in the warm, coastal waters of the Indian and Pacific oceans.

Do they live in groups?

Dugongs spend most of their time alone or in pairs, but they do sometimes gather in groups of 100!

How do dugongs talk to each other?

They squeak and chirp to send each other messages! Dugongs have good hearing.

Can dugongs breathe underwater?
No, they must come to the surface for air. They can hold their breath underwater for a long time though —up to 11 minutes!

Do they leap from the water?
No, instead they "stand" on their tails and poke their noses out of the water!

What other animals are they related to?
Strange as it may seem, dugongs are related to elephants!

SPEEDY SWIMMERS

Out in the open ocean, creatures often use speed
to catch prey—or to avoid predators.

How do they catch fish?
They have a long spike, or bill,
above their mouth, which they use
like a spear.

**How did sailfish get
their name?**
They are named after the
large, sail-like fin that
runs along their back.

Can tuna swim fast?
Yes they can! With their
streamlined bodies, tuna are
built for speed.

Can flying fish really fly?

Almost! Once out of the water, they spread out their fins and glide for about 45 seconds!

Can a sailfish swim far?

Yes! In its lifetime, a sailfish will swim the equivalent of eight times around the world.

ADVENTUROUS TURTLES

These beautiful reptiles live in warm
seas all over the world.

Why do sea turtles have shells?
Their tough shells protect turtles
from predators.

What do turtles eat?
Turtles eat creatures, such
as jellyfish and sea sponges,
using their sharp, beak-like
mouths. Chomp!

How many kinds of turtle are there?
There are seven different species (types) of
sea turtle. The largest is the leatherback. It
is much bigger than a person.

Where do turtles lay their eggs?
Female turtles swim hundreds of miles to the beach where they hatched to lay their own eggs.

What are baby turtles called?
They are called hatchlings! They crawl to the sea trying to avoid animals that hunt them, such as birds.

Can turtles breathe underwater?
No, but they can hold their breath and stay below the surface for hours at a time!

ADORABLE DOLPHINS

Bottlenose dolphins have powerful fins that make them speedy swimmers.

Can baby dolphins swim from birth?

Baby dolphins can swim just minutes after they are born! They stay close to their mothers for around six years.

What is a group of dolphins called?

A group of dolphins is called a pod. Living with other dolphins gives them protection from enemies. It also allows them to hunt for food as a team.

Where do dolphins live?
Bottlenose dolphins live in warm waters around the world.

Why do dolphins have blowholes on their heads?
Like whales, dolphins come to the surface to breathe air through their blowholes.

Can dolphins talk?
Not like we do, but dolphins click, squeak, and even bump heads to send all kinds of messages to each other.

151

MYSTERIOUS RAYS

With their wide, flattened bodies and long, thin tails, rays are unusual-looking fish.

Can mantas swim long distances?

Some types can! Giant manta rays can travel far across the open ocean.

Where do rays live?

Rays live in many of the world's oceans. Most live on the bottom of shallow seas.

How big is a giant manta?

Giant mantas can measure as wide as four people lying end to end!

Can mantas fly?

No, but they do flap their fins like wings to "fly" through the water, and sometimes they leap above the waves.

What do rays eat?
They eat tiny ocean creatures called plankton. The large flaps on either side of a manta's head push them into their mouth.

How do they hunt prey?
Electric rays can deliver a powerful electric shock. They use this to find food and to defend themselves.

INTO THE DEEP

As the ocean gets deeper, it also gets colder and darker. Strange creatures live down here.

Which deep ocean fish is like a light bulb?

Viperfish have large mouths with long, sharp teeth. Their bodies can make their own light!

Are there goblins in the deep sea?

No! But there are goblin sharks that use electricity to find food in the dark. Their jaws shoot out of their mouth to grab hold of prey.

Are there plants on the ocean floor?

No, the creatures that live here eat pieces of food that drift down from above—or each other!

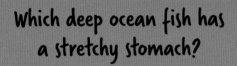

Why do anglerfish glow in the dark?

Anglerfish have a spine on their head called a lure. The lure glows in the dark, which attracts prey.

Which deep ocean fish has a stretchy stomach?

Black swallower fish have super-stretchy stomachs! They can gulp down creatures double their own size!

Which fish can stand?

Tripod fish! They use their three long, bony spines to "stand" on the seafloor, waiting for tiny creatures to swim by.

WONDERFUL WHALES

Blue whales live in every ocean on Earth.
They are the gentle giants of the sea.

How big are blue whales?

Enormous! Imagine a long line of
17 people swimming in a row—
that's how big they can be!

Do they have sharp teeth?

No, they don't. Instead of teeth,
blue whales have baleen plates,
which look a bit like combs.

What do blue whales eat?

They eat krill—tiny
shrimplike creatures that
gather in huge groups called
swarms. The swarms look
like pink clouds and can
contain millions of krill.

How much do they eat in a day?
Blue whales eat around four million krill every single day! Their baleen plates filter (strain) the krill from the water.

Were the dinosaurs bigger?
No, blue whales are the largest animals to live on Earth—ever!

How long can a blue whale stay under water?
These massive mammals can hold their breath under water for more than one hour.

BEAUTIFUL JELLYFISH

Jellyfish are found in every ocean on Earth. Some prefer warm seas, while others live in deep, cold waters.

Do jellyfish have skeletons?

Jellyfish are invertebrates, which means they don't have a backbone. They don't have a brain either!

What do you call a group of jellyfish?

A bloom!

Which jellyfish can create light?

Many jellyfish, such as these mauve stingers, are bioluminescent. This means their bodies can create light.

How do jellyfish catch prey?
They use their long, stinging tentacles to catch fish and tiny sea creatures.

Are jellyfish deadly?
Some kinds are extremely dangerous and are more venomous than any snake.

How big can they grow?
The largest jellyfish can grow to be bigger than a person. The tiniest can be smaller than your fingernail!

159

ICY-COLD WATERS

At the very top of Earth lies the chilly Arctic Ocean.
In the winter, most of the ocean is covered with ice.

How do Arctic animals stay warm?

Seals and walruses have a layer of fat
under their skin, called blubber, which
protects them from the cold.

What do seals eat?

Seals love to eat Arctic
cod. They dive deep
under the ice in search
of them.

Which type of whale looks like a unicorn?

A narwhal! The males have a
long, spiral tusk.

GIANT SQUID

Lurking in the ocean depths is a real-life sea monster.

How big is the giant squid?

Really big! A giant squid can be longer than a bus. They are the biggest invertebrates (animals without skeletons) in the world.

Do giant squid have predators?

The only known predators of giant squid are sperm whales. Many sperm whales have scars caused by giant squid suckers.

What do giant squid eat?
Giant squid eat fish and smaller squid. Their sharp beaks rip their meals apart.

How big are their eyes?
A giant squid's eyes are bigger than soccer balls! Good eyesight helps the squid scan the dark ocean for food.

How many arms does a giant squid have?
Giant squid have eight long arms and two tentacles covered with suckers. The suckers help them grab hold of prey.

INCREDIBLE PENGUINS

These birds cannot fly, but they are great swimmers and divers.

Where do penguins live?

Penguins are found in the southern part of the world. These emperor penguins live in Antarctica, the coldest place on Earth.

Can penguins glide on ice?

Yes, they can! Emperor penguins slide on their bellies across the ice and into the water. They dive deep down to search for fish and squid to eat.

Do penguins flock together?

Penguins do live together in groups, yes, but these are called colonies, not flocks.

Do penguins have special feathers?

Yes, penguins have oily feathers that keep them warm and dry in the cold water.

Why do penguins huddle?

To keep warm! Winters in the Antarctic are freezing. The ones in the middle of the huddle are the coziest!

Can penguins breathe under water?

No, they can't—but they can hold their breath for more than half an hour.

OCEAN ANIMALS QUIZ

How well do you remember facts about ocean creatures?
Decide if these sentences are true or false, then check your
answers on page 256.

1 Some fish living in deep, dark water can make their own light.

2 Sea otters live in groups.

3 Tiger sharks are small, about the size of a banana.

4. Blue whales are bigger than any of the dinosaurs.

5 Pelicans catch fish by scooping them up in their beaks.

6. Jellyfish are mammals.

7 To escape predators, pocupine fish hide in coral reefs.

8 Seahorses eat only one meal every week.

SPACE

STARRY NIGHT

Look up! There are so many stars in the sky. No one could count them all. It would take too long!

When do the stars come out?

Twinkling dots of light called stars come out after dark.

Is there a bear in the sky?

Not a real bear! But if you connect the starry dots into groups, you can make pictures, such as a bear.

How can I see stars more clearly?

Look through a telescope, and stars will seem bigger and brighter.

What is a star?

A star is a huge ball of hot gas that burns fiercely and gives off lots of light.

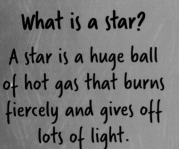

Is the Sun a star?

Yes, the Sun is a star. It looks different from the stars we see at night because it is much closer to us.

How far away are the other stars?

They are extremely far away! It would take thousands of years to travel to the nearest one.

How old are they?

Some stars are billions of years old. That's a lot of birthdays!

THE STARS ABOVE US

Our nearest star, the Sun, is just one of many billions of stars that make up the Milky Way. The Milky Way is a group of stars called a galaxy.

Can we see the Milky Way from Earth?

Yes! On a very clear night, we can see this beautiful blanket of stars.

Does it have any other names?

It does! Ancient Romans called it the "road of milk," and ancient Greeks named it the "milky circle."

Are there lots of galaxies?

Yes—there are many, many more galaxies filled with all kinds of different stars.

What are constellations?
Constellations are star patterns in the sky, such as the Great Bear. You can use star maps to find them.

Can I see a constellation?
On a clear night, you may be able to see Orion. This famous constellation can be seen throughout the whole world.

Earth is here

Why are constellations useful?
Because they help us recognize and find certain stars, for example the North Star, which explorers used to find their way.

OUR AMAZING UNIVERSE

When we look up into space, we are looking out into the Universe. It's billions of years old!

What actually is the Universe?

The Universe is EVERYTHING, including all the stars and planets and things we can see. It also includes all the things we can't see.

Is the Universe growing?

Yes, the Universe is growing outward,
getting bigger all the time.

What is the Big Bang?

The Big Bang is the name
experts use to describe
the moment the Universe
first formed in a huge
explosion.

**Is Earth on the edge of
the Universe?**

We don't know—scientists
are trying to pinpoint our
location.

173

THE SOLAR SYSTEM

The solar system is the planets, moons, and other space objects moving around our Sun.

Asteroid belt

Earth

Which planets are made of rock?

Earth, Mercury, Venus, and Mars are the rocky planets.

Venus

Mercury

SUN

Where is the Sun in the solar system?

It is right in the middle!

Why don't the planets zoom off into space?

The Sun pulls the solar system's planets toward it. This keeps the planets from zooming off into outer space.

Jupiter

What are orbits?
Orbits are the invisible paths that the planets follow around the Sun.

Neptune

Are orbits circles?
No, planets have oval-shaped orbits.

Uranus

Which planets are made of gas?
Jupiter, Saturn, Uranus, and Neptune are mostly made up of gases, which means we can't land on their surface.

Mars

Saturn

HOW BIG?

Here are all of the planets
in our solar system.
Some of them are
unimaginably big.

← Jupiter

**Which is the biggest
planet?**

Jupiter! It is more
than ten times the size
of Earth.

Saturn →

**How much wider is Saturn
than Earth?**

It is nine times as wide. Wow!

Uranus

Neptune

Are any of the planets larger than the Sun?

No—the Sun is by far the biggest object in our solar system—it's nearly ten times wider than the next biggest!

Moon

Earth

SUN

Which are the smallest planets?

The four closest planets to the Sun (Mercury, Venus, Earth, and Mars) are the four smallest planets, too.

Mars

Venus

Which planet is the closest to the Sun?

Mercury is the closest. It circles the Sun more quickly than all the other planets.

Mercury

177

OUR LIFE-GIVING STAR

The Sun, our closest star, is an enormous ball of burning hot gas in space.

Why do we need the Sun to survive?

One of the main reasons we have life on Earth is the Sun—it gives us light and warmth.

What is a solar flare?

Solar flares are sudden bright flashes on the Sun's surface. The hot gas in the Sun is always moving.

How much bigger is the Sun than Earth?

More than one million planet Earths would fit inside the Sun. It's enormous!

Is the Sun spotty?

Yes! The darker, cooler areas are sunspots.

What are prominences?

They are huge loops that burst out of the Sun and into space.

Is there any wind on the Sun?

Yes—the Sun gives off something called solar wind. These are gases that stream out into space.

What is an eclipse?

When our Moon moves past the Sun, it makes a shadow fall on Earth. This is an eclipse.

MERCURY: THE WRINKLY PLANET

The closest planet to the Sun, Mercury, is the smallest planet in our solar system and is only a little bigger than Earth's Moon.

How long is one year on Mercury?

One year on Mercury lasts the same amount of time as roughly three months on Earth!

How did Mercury get its name?

It is named after the Roman god Mercury, a messenger who could travel at very fast speeds.

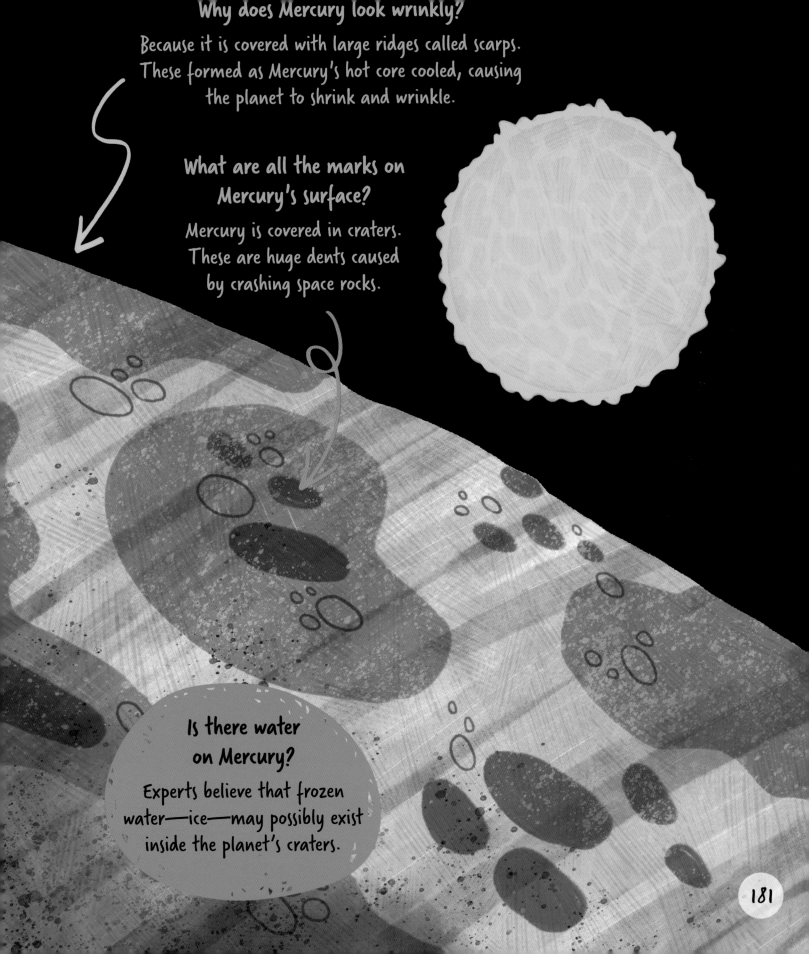

Why does Mercury look wrinkly?

Because it is covered with large ridges called scarps.
These formed as Mercury's hot core cooled, causing
the planet to shrink and wrinkle.

**What are all the marks on
Mercury's surface?**

Mercury is covered in craters.
These are huge dents caused
by crashing space rocks.

**Is there water
on Mercury?**

Experts believe that frozen
water—ice—may possibly exist
inside the planet's craters.

181

VENUS: OUR SISTER PLANET

Venus, the second planet from the
Sun, is very similar in size to Earth
and is also rocky.

Could humans live on Venus?

Definitely not. Venus is much hotter than
Earth—we couldn't survive the heat!

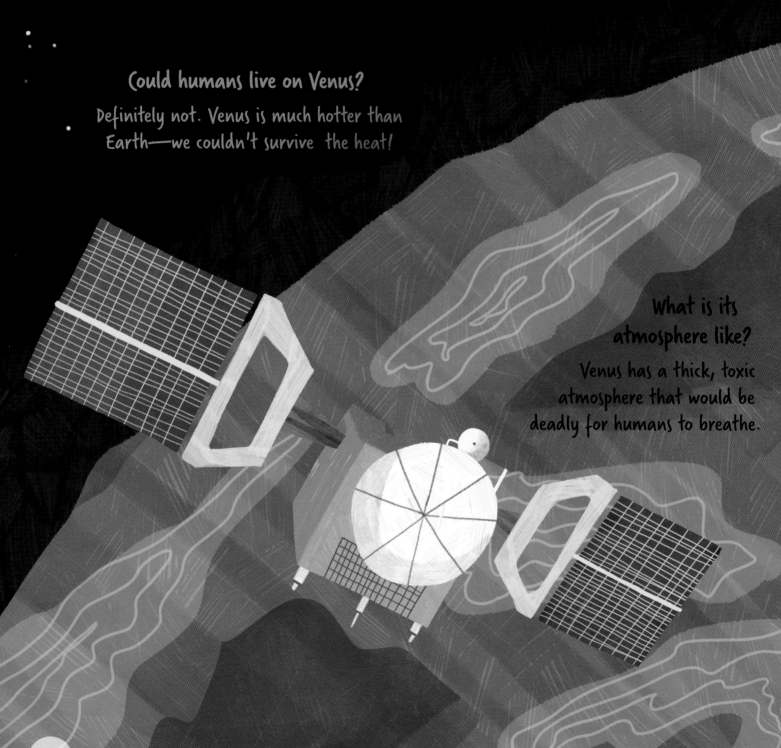

**What is its
atmosphere like?**

Venus has a thick, toxic
atmosphere that would be
deadly for humans to breathe.

Can I see Venus?

Yes! It can be seen from Earth on a clear night. Its light is steady, not twinkly like the stars.

How long is a day on Venus?

One day on Venus is very long—the same as 243 Earth days!

How did Venus get its name?

Venus is named after the Roman goddess of love and beauty.

What is the atmosphere?

It is the protective layer of gases that covers the planet like a blanket. It keeps us safe from harmful Sun rays.

Is Earth one of the biggest planets?

Earth is the biggest rocky planet, but it is much smaller than the gas planets.

184

EARTH: OUR HOME PLANET

The largest rocky planet, and third planet from the Sun, is our home—planet Earth.

Why is Earth called a goldilocks planet?

Because it is not too hot and not too cold—conditions here are "just right" for life to exist.

What are rockets?

Rockets are amazing space machines that can leave Earth and travel into space. They go to satellites, the Moon, or distant planets!

MOON: LUNAR LIFE

The Moon is a huge ball of space rock orbiting Earth.

What is the Moon?

The Moon is a natural satellite. A satellite is a space object that follows a path around a planet.

How old is the Moon?

Scientists think that the Moon may have formed billions of years ago.

Have humans been to the Moon?

Yes—the Moon is the only place in space where humans have actually set foot!

Why does the Moon look different every few days?

Because different parts of it are lit up by the Sun every couple of days. These changes are called phases.

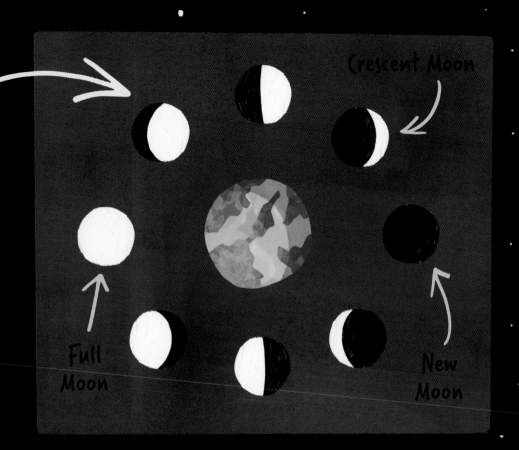

Crescent Moon

Full Moon

New Moon

Each year, the Moon moves a little farther away from us.

What are the marks on the Moon?

Like Mercury, the Moon has many craters—dents caused by space rock crashing into the surface. Many can be spotted from Earth.

Do other planets have moons?

Some other planets have moons, yes, but not all. Our Moon is the fifth largest in our solar system!

187

MARS: THE RED PLANET

The fourth planet from the Sun, Mars, is also known as the red planet. Its rocky surface is covered in an orange-red dust.

How big is Mars?

Named after the Roman god of war, Mars is about half the size of Earth.

Is there water on Mars?

Yes, but only at its polar ice caps. It is thought that the planet once had rivers, lakes, and seas.

Can I move to Mars?

It would be very hard for people to live on this freezing-cold planet. Yet scientists are trying to find out if it might be possible in the future!

Can we see Mars from Earth?

Yes! Sometimes we can see Mars glowing in the night sky. It looks orange-red.

What is Olympus Mons?

Olympus Mons is the highest mountain in the solar system, and it is found on Mars. It is almost three times as high as the highest mountain on Earth.

How do we know so much about Mars?

Special spacecraft called rovers have been to the surface of Mars to collect and send information back to Earth.

189

How did Jupiter get its name?

Jupiter is named after the Roman king of the gods.

What makes the swirly pattern on its surface?

The swirls on Jupiter's outer surface are made of up gases. They may look nice, but they would be deadly to breathe!

What is the Great Red Spot?

There are many storms on Jupiter, and one of them is called the Great Red Spot. This huge hurricane has been going on for almost 200 years!

JUPITER: THE BIGGEST OF ALL

Jupiter, the fifth planet from the Sun, is the largest planet in our solar system.

Could I stand on the surface of Jupiter?

It would be impossible to stand on the surface of this great gas giant because it isn't solid!

How many moons does Jupiter have?

Jupiter has an incredible 67 moons!

Which is its biggest moon?

The largest of all, Ganymede, is even bigger than Mercury.

SATURN: THE JEWEL OF THE SOLAR SYSTEM

Saturn is the sixth planet from the Sun. It is famous for the many sparkling rings that circle around its middle.

What are Saturn's rings made up of?

Broken pieces of icy space rock! They were first spotted by astronomer Galileo hundreds of years ago.

Which of Saturn's moons is the biggest?

Titan. It is the second-biggest moon in the entire solar system.

What is Saturn named after?

It is named after the god of farming in ancient Rome.

How is Saturn similar to Jupiter?

Like Jupiter, the beautiful planet Saturn is a gas giant.

Why is Titan a little bit like Earth?

Titan is the only other space object with clouds like Earth. It also has its own atmosphere, like a planet.

How heavy is Saturn?

As Saturn is made of gas, it is very light. If it was placed in a GIANT bowl of water, it would float! Wow!

URANUS: THE ICE GIANT

Uranus is the seventh planet from the Sun and the third gas giant. Like Saturn, it too has rings.

Why is Uranus so icy?

This gas giant is made up of extremely cold gases.

Can you see Uranus from Earth?

Only by telescope. It is far too small to be seen by the naked human eye.

Has Uranus tipped over?

No—Uranus' rings run from its top to its bottom, which makes it look like it has fallen over!

How did Uranus get its name?

It was named after a Greek god of the sky.

Does Uranus have moons?

Yes! It has 27. One of its most famous, named Miranda, is covered in icy canyons.

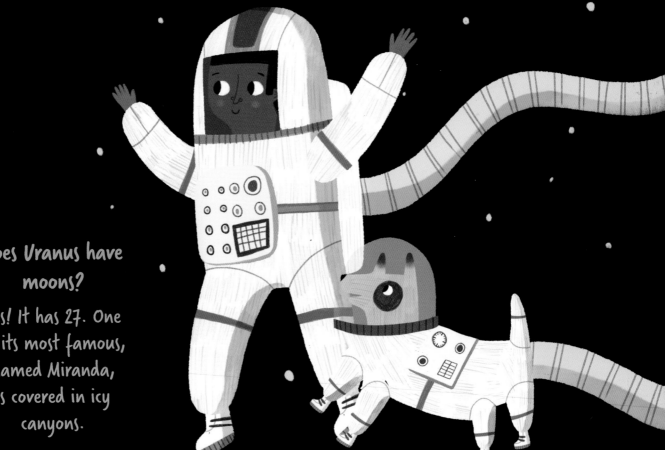

NEPTUNE: THE BLUE PLANET

At the edge of our solar system is Neptune, the eighth planet.
It is also the final gas giant.

What's the weather like on Neptune?

Very windy! Its winds reach far higher speeds than those on Earth.

How did Neptune get its name?

Neptune is named after the Roman god of the sea. Through a telescope, Neptune glows a beautiful bright blue.

What is Neptune's biggest moon?

Neptune's biggest moon is Triton. Unusually, it spins in the opposite direction to all of Neptune's other moons.

Does Neptune have rings?

It does! Neptune has rings running around its middle, perhaps made from smashed-up space rock.

DWARF PLANETS

A dwarf planet is similar to a true planet in many ways.

Are dwarf planets small?

Yes—they are much smaller than the eight main planets.

Do dwarf planets orbit the Sun?

Yes, just like the main planets, dwarf planets travel around the Sun.

Which dwarf planet is farthest from the Sun?

Eris. It is three times as far from the Sun as Pluto.

Does Eris have a moon?

Yes! It s called Dysnomia.

Is Pluto a dwarf planet?

Yes! We used to think it was a main planet, but scientists decided it was the largest of the dwarf planets instead.

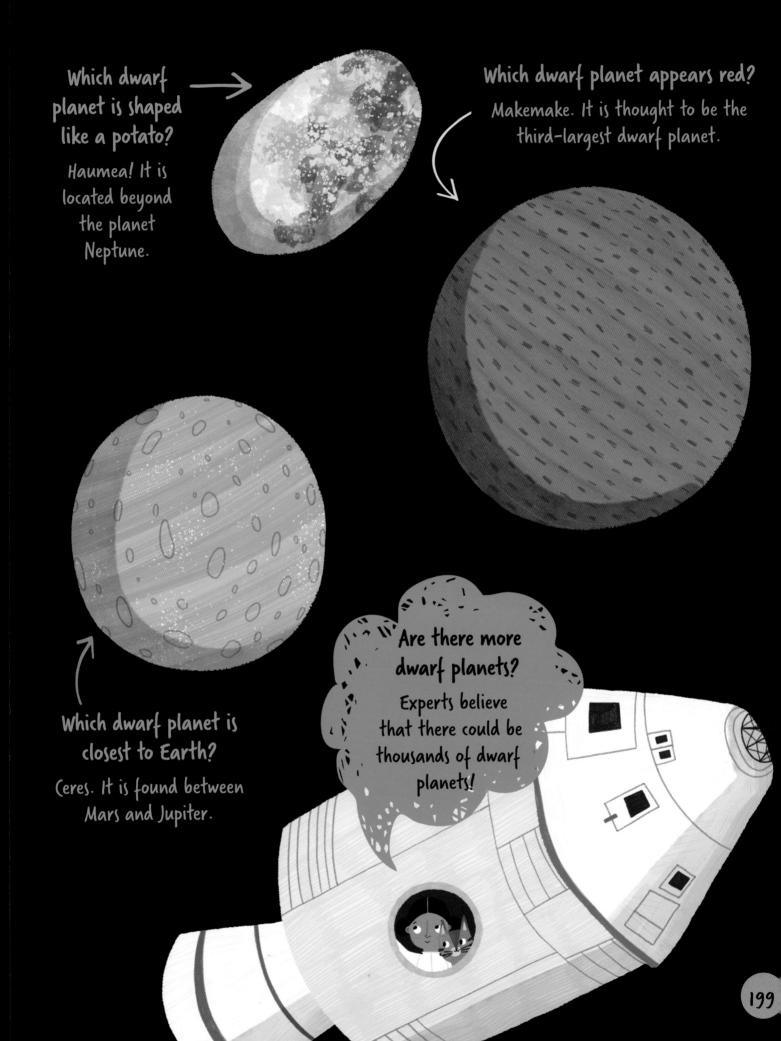

Which dwarf planet is shaped like a potato?

Haumea! It is located beyond the planet Neptune.

Which dwarf planet appears red?

Makemake. It is thought to be the third-largest dwarf planet.

Which dwarf planet is closest to Earth?

Ceres. It is found between Mars and Jupiter.

Are there more dwarf planets?

Experts believe that there could be thousands of dwarf planets!

COMETS, ASTEROIDS, AND METEORS

As well as planets and moons, space is full of different kinds of space rock.

What is a comet?

Comets are big pieces of rock and ice that whirl around the Sun.

Do comets have tails?

Yes! They leave behind long trails of gas called tails. These tails can be thousands of miles long.

How big are asteroids?

Asteroids are pieces of space rock that can be just a few feet in length—or big enough to have their own moons.

What is the asteroid belt?

It is a huge band of asteroids located between Mars and Jupiter.

Can an asteroid be as large as a planet?

Yes! Vesta is one of the largest asteroids. It is like a small, rocky planet.

What does space rock look like from space?

This picture shows us what different kinds of rock looks like close up.

Comet

Earth

Meteors

Asteroid

What are meteors?

Meteors are smaller pieces of rock. If they come close to the Earth, they burn up as they fall to the ground. Then, they are known as shooting stars.

SPACE TELESCOPES

Telescopes let us see farther into space than we can see with just our eyes. Some are based on Earth, but some have been sent into space.

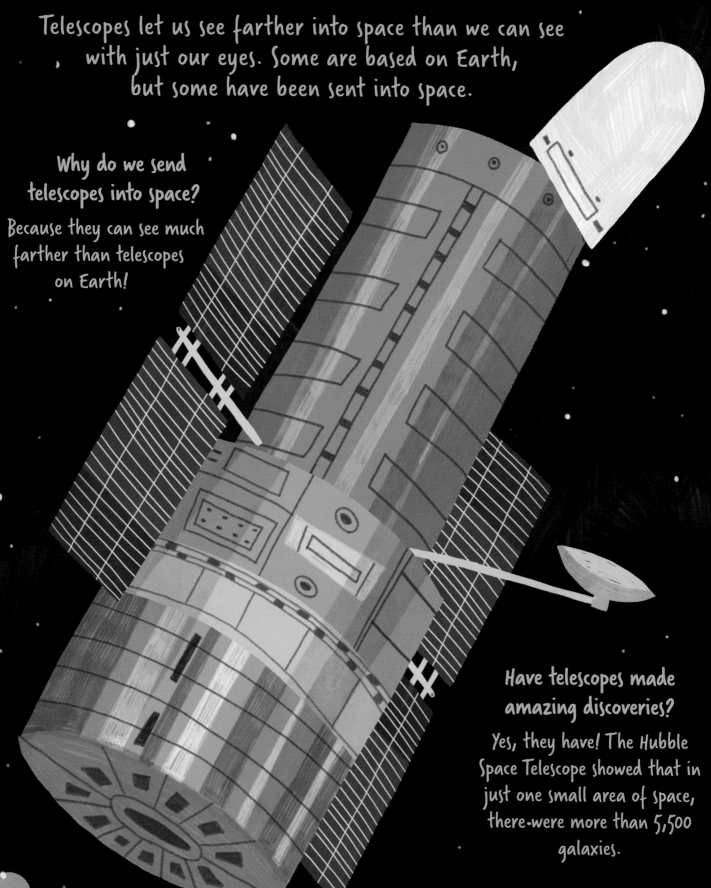

Why do we send telescopes into space?

Because they can see much farther than telescopes on Earth!

Have telescopes made amazing discoveries?

Yes, they have! The Hubble Space Telescope showed that in just one small area of space, there were more than 5,500 galaxies.

SPACE TRAVEL

To send a spacecraft into space, scientists use a launch vehicle, or rocket.

How do rockets leave Earth?

Using powerful engines that help them reach speeds fast enough to leave Earth's atmosphere.

How are they powered?

They burn lots of fuel, which gives them enough energy to move.

Have astronauts been to Mars?

Not yet, but the new Space Launch System (SLS) will soon be in use. It may take astronauts to Mars for the first time ever.

Where is the best place to launch a rocket?

It is easiest to launch a rocket into space from near the equator, the invisible line around the middle of Earth.

The Space Shuttle

Does the Space Shuttle still fly?
No, not any more. Now retired, it flew 135 missions and carried seven astronauts each time.

Have any rockets left our solar system?

Two spacecraft, Voyager 1 and Voyager 2, have left the planets of our solar system far behind. Incredibly, they are still sending back information to Earth.

THE INTERNATIONAL SPACE STATION

Many nations from across the world came together to build this amazing space station.

Where is the International Space Station?

The International Space Station (ISS) is above Earth! It travels around our planet multiple times per day.

Do astronauts eat in space?

Of course! Astronauts eat three meals a day. They eat with knives and forks, or chopsticks, like we do on Earth.

...nauts could do scientific experiments in space. They look at what happens to our bodies when we are in space, for example.

How big is the ISS?

As long as a football stadium! Sometimes it can be seen zooming across the sky like a fast-moving plane.

Do astronauts exercise in space?

They do! On the ISS, astronauts have to exercise for two hours each day to stay fit. Otherwise, their muscles and bones get weak.

SPACE QUIZ

How well do you remember facts about space? Decide if these sentences are true or false, then check your answers on page 256.

1 The planet Venus can be seen from Earth.

2 Mercury is the farthest planet from the Sun.

3 Astronauts have visited Mars.

4 Asteroids can be large enough to have their own moons.

5 There are six planets circling our Sun.

6 The Great Red Spot is a storm on Jupiter.

7 A comet is a large piece of rock and ice.

8 Saturn does not have any moons.

HOW THINGS WORK

WHAT MAKES BICYCLES GO?

Bicycles are machines that help us get from one place to another.

BRAKE

HANDLEBARS

What do the handlebars do?
They change the direction of the front wheel.

How do you stop moving?
You squeeze the brake to make little pads push against the wheels, which stops them from turning.

GEAR

PEDAL

CHAIN

How do pedals work?

When you push down on the pedals with your feet, a chain is dragged around the bicyle's gears. This turns the back wheel.

WHEEL

How do bikes move forward?

When the back wheel turns, it pushes the bicycle forward and forces the front wheel to turn.

HOW DO SHOES STAY FASTENED?

There are simple but clever inventions we use to fasten our shoes.

Do all shoes have hook-and-loop fastenings?

Children's shoes ofen have hook-and-loop fasteners as they are easy to use. But shoes can also be fastened with laces or buckles.

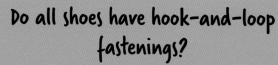

213

HOW DO DISHWASHERS CLEAN DISHES?

Dishwashers are machines that clean and rinse your dirty dishes.

Are dishwashers new inventions?

No, they were invented more than 130 years ago. They worked in a similar way to the ones we use today!

SOAP COMPARTMENT

What happens inside a dishwasher?

A pump heats up clean water and pushes it into spray arms, which turn to spray clean water onto the dishes. Once the dishes are clean, dirty water is drained away.

SPRAY ARM

PUMP

What do they need to work?

Dishwashers need electricity and water.

Does it use soap?

Yes! A soap compartment pops open during the wash. The soap mixes with the water in the machine.

HOW DOES A SPACECRAFT LAUNCH?

Launch vehicles are used to send spacecraft and satellites into space. They need rocket power to get there.

Does all of the launch vehicle go into space?

No, just the spacecraft. This is contained inside a nose cone called the payload fairing.

What happens to the rocket?

Once a rocket has burned all of its fuel, it drops back to Earth. Some rockets can be collected and used again.

PAYLOAD FAIRING

MAIN ROCKET

ROCKET BOOSTER

What happens inside the rocket?

Inside the rocket, oxygen (found in the air we breathe) is mixed with fuel in the rocket's combustion chamber.

How does this launch the rocket?

It causes an explosion! Waste gases blast out and down from the rocket. This forces the rocket up!

INSIDE MAIN ROCKET

FUEL

LIQUID OXYGEN

COMBUSTION CHAMBER →

WHAT KEEPS A LOCK LOCKED?

We keep our homes safe by locking the doors.

What is a deadbolt?

A piece of metal inside a lock that goes in and out as the key is turned.

Are all keys the same?

No, each key has parts cut out of it in a unique pattern to match the lock.

How does a deadbolt move?

Inside the lock are a set of levers, which let the deadbolt move— but only when the right key is placed inside the lock.

DEADBOLT OUTSIDE LOCK

LEVERS

LOCKED

DEADBOLT INSIDE LOCK

UNLOCKED

How does the door lock?

When the deadbolt slides into the slot in the door frame, it holds the door in place. When the deadbolt is inside the lock, the door can open.

HOW DOES A PHONE MAKE A CALL?

Phones are a handy way to keep in touch with friends and family.

Does my phone have a microphone?

Yes! A tiny microphone inside the phone picks up your voice when you speak. It turns the sounds into an electrical signal.

What happens next?

The phone turns the signal into radio waves. Radio waves are invisible waves of energy that can travel through air and space.

How does my voice reach my friend's phone?

(1) A structure at a base station receives the radio waves from your phone.

(2) Then, the base station sends the radio waves to a central station in the area.

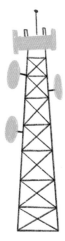

(5) Finally, their phone receives the radio waves and changes them back into sounds!

(3) The central station sends the radio waves to a base station close to your friend.

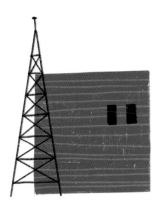

(4) That base station sends the radio waves to their phone.

HOW DOES A VACUUM CLEANER WORK?

A vacuum cleaner sucks up dust and dirt from your floor.

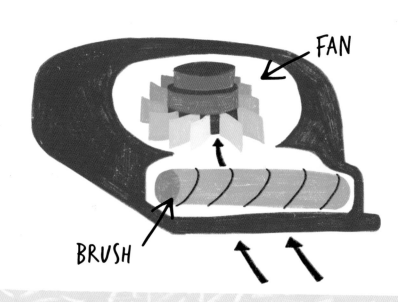

FAN

BRUSH

What happens inside the vacuum?

A spinning brush loosens all the dust and dirt from the floor, then a fan sucks up the dirty air through a pipe and into the container. Here, the dirt and dust passes through a filter. Only clean air flows out.

What happens when the vacuum is full?

When the container is full of dust and dirt, it needs to be emptied, ready for next time.

Are there bags inside vacuums?

Some vacuum cleaners have bags that the dirt goes into, while others have see-through containers. But they all work in the same way!

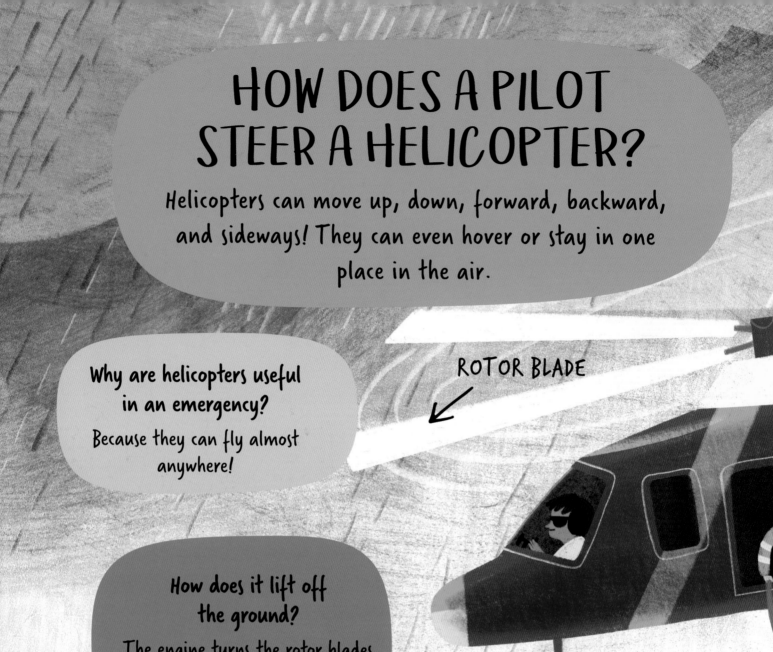

HOW DOES A PILOT STEER A HELICOPTER?

Helicopters can move up, down, forward, backward, and sideways! They can even hover or stay in one place in the air.

Why are helicopters useful in an emergency?

Because they can fly almost anywhere!

ROTOR BLADE

How does it lift off the ground?

The engine turns the rotor blades really fast to lift the helicopter into the air.

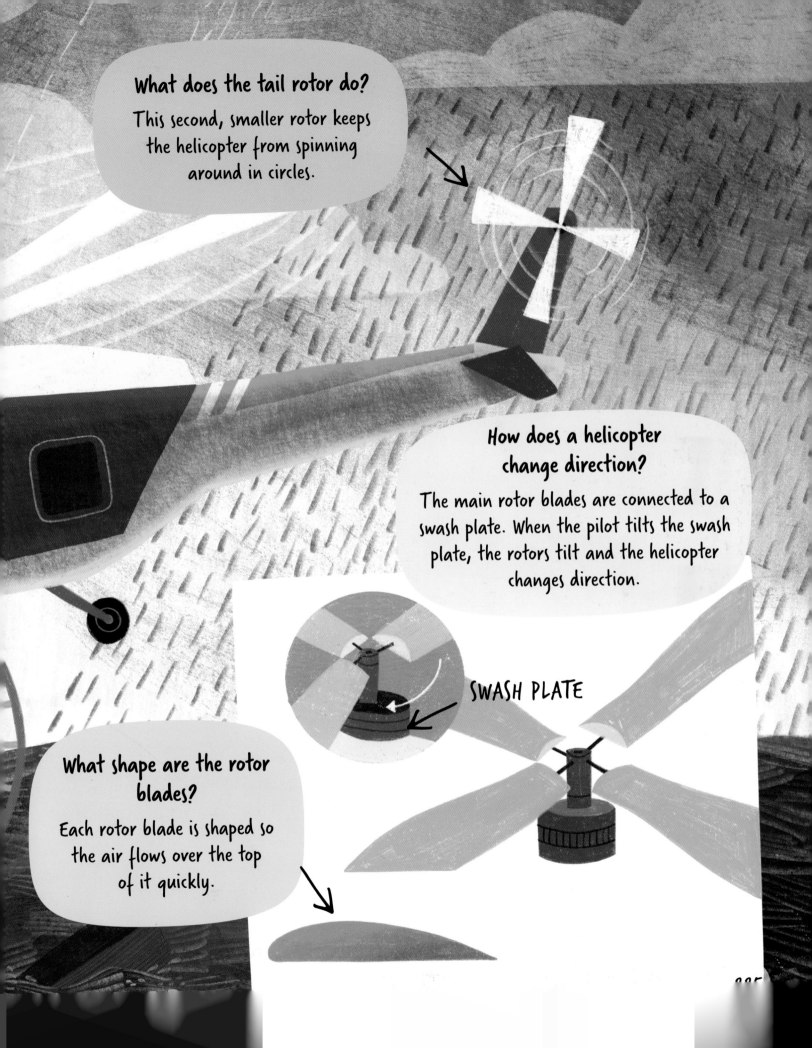

What does the tail rotor do?
This second, smaller rotor keeps the helicopter from spinning around in circles.

How does a helicopter change direction?
The main rotor blades are connected to a swash plate. When the pilot tilts the swash plate, the rotors tilt and the helicopter changes direction.

SWASH PLATE

What shape are the rotor blades?
Each rotor blade is shaped so the air flows over the top of it quickly.

HOW DO PENS MAKE MARKS?

Hundreds of years ago, people wrote and drew pictures using the tip of a feather dipped in ink. It was very messy!

When were ballpoint pens invented?

About 90 years ago, in the 1930s!

Is there a ball in a ballpoint pen?

Yes! The tip of a ballpoint pen contains a tiny ball.

How does a ballpoint pen work?

As you push the pen across paper, the ball rolls around and gets coated with ink from a tube inside the pen. A line of ink is left on the paper.

How do felt-tips work?

The nib (tip) of a felt-tip pen is made from nylon. The nib soaks up ink from the main part of the pen.

227

HOW DOES A COMPUTER WORK?

A computer, such as a laptop or tablet, is a machine that follows a set of instructions. It makes calculations and stores information.

What is hardware?
The outside parts of a computer that you can touch!

How do we give computers information?
We do this by using the keyboard, mouse, camera, or touchscreen.

What is a program?

A program is a set of instructions a computer follows to complete a task. Together, programs are called software.

What are output devices?

Screens, printers, and speakers are output devices.

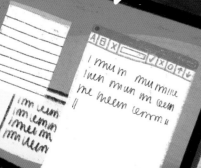

Which part of the computer makes decisions?

Inside the computer, a device called a processor receives the information and decides what to do next.

Which part of the computer is like a brain?

The processor! It deals with all the information that goes into and out of the computer. It is small but very powerful.

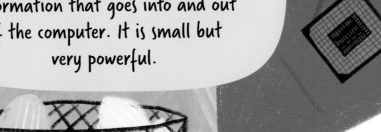

HOW DOES AN ONLINE GAME WORK?

Online games send messages through the Internet. The Internet is a system that connects millions of computers around the world.

How do their computers "talk" to each other?

They use the Internet! Information, such as words, pictures, and videos can be sent from one computer to another this way.

What are online games?

These games use the Internet to connect computers. Players can share their moves in the game.

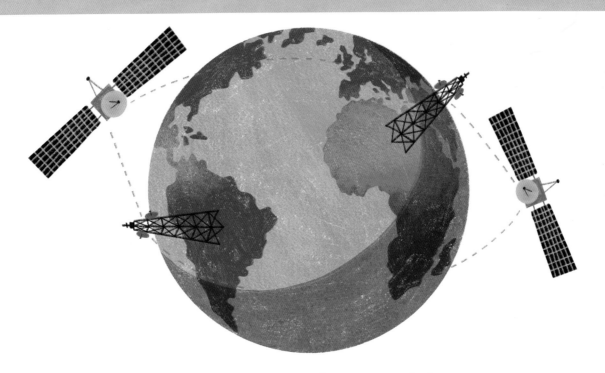

How are computers connected?

There are different ways. Some are linked by cables underground. Some use radio waves or connect to satellites—this is called a wireless connection.

What are websites?

Websites are places where people can find information, do their shopping, and play games. Computers use the Internet to access websites.

WHAT MAKES A CAR MOVE?

Inside every car is an engine, which makes the car go.

How do cars move?

Some cars use liquid fuel to power the engine. Burning the fuel moves parts called pistons up and down. Their movement is used to turn the wheels.

Do all cars use liquid fuel?

Not all cars. Some are powered by electricity, which is stored in a battery. Electric cars need to be plugged in to "charging points" to charge the battery.

232

How do car wheels turn?

(1) As the pistons move up and down, they turn a part called the crankshaft.

PISTONS

WHEEL

CRANKSHAFT

DRIVESHAFT

(2) The crankshaft connects to a part called the driveshaft.

(3) The driveshaft turns the wheels around, so the car moves forward.

HOW DOES A MICROWAVE OVEN COOK FOOD?

If you want a quick, hot meal, put it in the microwave ...
it will be ready in minutes!

Are microwaves the same as regular ovens?

No, regular ovens cook by heating up the air around the food. In a microwave oven, food is cooked from the inside out.

Which heats food quicker, a microwave or a regular oven?

For most foods, a microwave is much quicker!

What actually are "microwaves?"

They are waves of energy made by a special part inside the machine called a magnetron. The microwaves make particles (very tiny parts) of water inside the food move quickly. This cooks the food.

Why does the microwave need a fan?

A spinning fan bounces the microwaves around the inside of the oven and into the food.

MAGNETRON

235

HOW DOES A PIANO PLAY A TUNE?

A piano is a musical instrument with many strings inside. When you press a key, it makes the strings vibrate.

STRINGS

How do guitars make sounds?

A guitar player plucks or strums the strings!

How are sounds created?

We hear sounds when an object vibrates, or makes small movements back and forth quickly. Musical instruments work by making vibrations in the air in different ways.

How many strings does a piano have?

A piano can have around 230 strings. They are different lengths and thicknesses.

Why are piano strings different?

To make different notes. Short strings make high notes, and long strings make low notes!

Do pianos have hammers inside?

Yes! When a piano key is pressed, a lever pushes a tiny hammer inside.

What does the hammer do?

The hammer hits a string, which vibrates, making a sound. When the key is let go, a part called the damper moves down to stop the sound.

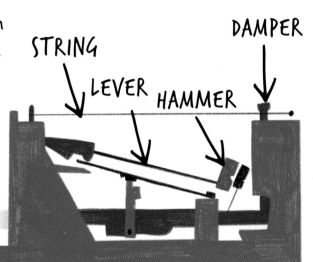

KEY

STRING

LEVER

DAMPER

HAMMER

WHAT MAKES A TOILET FLUSH?

When you pull the flush handle, parts inside a toilet work together to take away dirty water and replace it with clean water.

What's inside the toilet cistern?

The toilet cistern, or tank, is filled with clean water. Parts called valves let water into the cistern. They also stop the water when it is full.

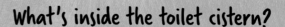

CISTERN

VALVES

FLUSH HANDLE

BOWL

What happens when I press the flush handle?

The cistern opens and water travels into the toilet bowl. Then clean water pushes the dirty waste water out through the waste pipe.

WASTE PIPE

Where does clean water come from?
Clean water is pumped through large pipes underground. Water flows through smaller pipes into our homes.

Where does the waste go?
Waste (dirty) water flows out through different pipes into drains. It goes to treatment plants to be cleaned and used again.

HOW DO TRAINS STAY ON THE TRACKS?

Trains can be powered by steam, electricity, or diesel fuel. But all types of trains travel along tracks.

What are rails?

They are the part of the track that the train travels along. This means they have to be made of steel, a very strong metal.

Do trains have wheels?

Yes! The wheels on each side of a train car are attached to a metal rod called an axle.

What does the axle do?

The axle keeps the wheels moving together and turning at the same speed.

How do the wheels stay on the rail?

Each wheel has a rim called a flange. The flanges are slotted on the inside of the rail, which keeps them from moving outward—and coming off the rail.

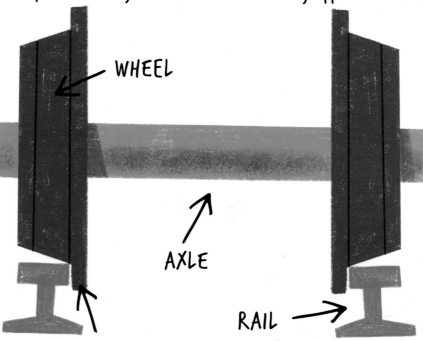

WHEEL

AXLE

RAIL

FLANGE

WHAT MAKES A HOT-AIR BALLOON GO UP?

Hot-air balloons are a beautiful sight, but how do they work?

Do hot-air balloons have engines?

No, they use something called a burner to fly.

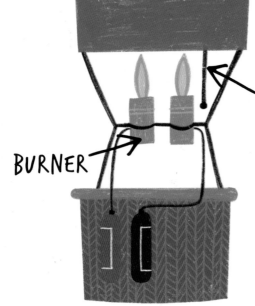

BURNER

CORD

How does the burner work?

When the pilot turns on the burner, it heats up the air inside the balloon. Hot air is lighter than the cold air outside, so the balloon floats up.

How does a balloon come back down to Earth?

The pilot pulls a cord that opens a flap at the top of the balloon. This lets out some hot air, which makes the balloon go down.

Are all balloons the same size?

No, they can be different shapes and sizes—some are even shaped like a teddy bear!

What is the envelope?

The rounded balloon part. It is made of tough fabric and filled with air.

Where does the pilot stand?

There is a basket underneath the envelope that carries the pilot—and any passengers!

243

HOW DOES A HAIR DRYER DRY MY HAIR?

Hair dryers blow out hot air to dry your wet hair in minutes.

What powers a hair dryer?
Hair dryers need electricity to work.

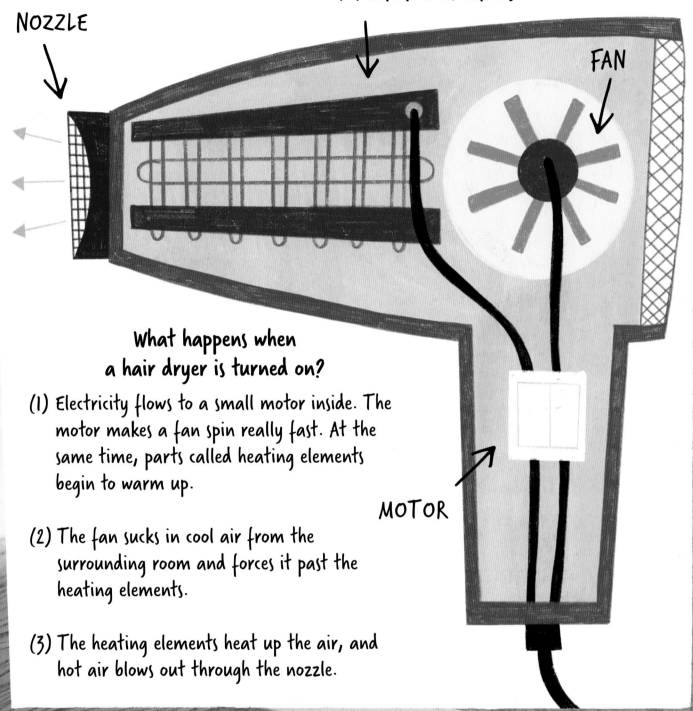

NOZZLE

HEATING ELEMENTS

FAN

MOTOR

What happens when a hair dryer is turned on?

(1) Electricity flows to a small motor inside. The motor makes a fan spin really fast. At the same time, parts called heating elements begin to warm up.

(2) The fan sucks in cool air from the surrounding room and forces it past the heating elements.

(3) The heating elements heat up the air, and hot air blows out through the nozzle.

HOW DO REFRIGERATORS KEEP FOOD FRESH?

The inside of a refrigerator keeps food cool so it lasts longer and less is wasted.

How does a refrigerator work?

It's all to do with something called a "refrigerant." The refrigerant travels around and around the machine's pipes. It changes from a liquid to a gas—and back again!

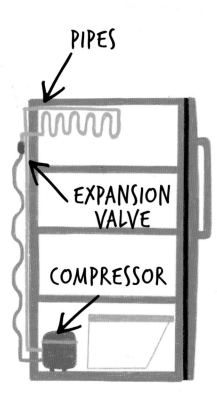

PIPES

EXPANSION VALVE

COMPRESSOR

How does the refrigerant become a gas?

A part called the "expansion valve" changes the refrigerant from a liquid into a gas. As this gas flows through the pipes on the inside of the refrigerator, it takes away the heat. The refrigerator becomes cooler.

What happens to the gas?

It leaves the inside part of the refrigerator and flows through a pump called a compressor. This squeezes the refrigerant, turning it back into a liquid. The heat is released through the pipes at the back and into the air.

What happens then?

The refrigerant flows back up to the expansion valve, ready to start all over again.

WHAT MAKES A CLOCK TICK?

Clocks are machines that tell us what time of day it is.

What do mechanical clocks look like?

A traditional mechanical clock has a face where the numbers are. The hands show the hours and minutes.

How do the hands move?

Inside the clock, weights and cogs work together to move the hands.

What are cogs?

Cogs are special wheels edged with teeth.

PENDULUM

ESCAPEMENT

COG

TOOTH

WEIGHT

How do the cogs move?

A part called the "escapement" allows the cogs to turn, one tooth at a time. A swinging weight called a pendulum controls how fast the teeth pass through the escapement.

Why do clocks tick?

As each tooth moves through the escapement, it creates a ticking sound.

How are clocks powered?

They run on the energy that is stored in the pendulum. To create the energy, the clock must be wound regularly.

Are all clocks mechanical?

No, some are electrical. Electrical clocks are powered by electricity. They often use batteries.

HOW THINGS WORK QUIZ

How well do you remember facts about how machines and other things work? Decide if these sentences are true or false, then check your answers on page 256.

1 Bicycle pedals are connected to a pendulum.

2 Dishwashers need electricity and water to work.

3 In a microwave oven, food is cooked from the inside.

4 A hot-air balloon uses a burner to make it fly.

5 Hairdryers need water to work.

6 Helicopters can only fly forward.

7 Musical instruments work by making vibrations
in the air in different ways.

8 Trains do not have wheels.

GLOSSARY

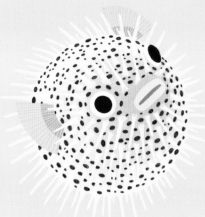

Algae plantlike living things, usually found in water.

Antenna a pair of feelers on the heads of many creepy-crawlies.

Asteroid a small, rocky space object.

Atmosphere a shell of gases around a planet, star, or other object.

Avalanche a huge amount of snow, ice, or rocks falling quickly down a mountain.

Battery a means of storing electricity.

Bioluminescence an animal's ability to make light within its own body.

Blow hole the hole on top of a whale or dolphin's head, which is used for breathing.

Camouflage when an animal's fur or skin copies the patterns from nature to help them hide from predators.

Canopy the thick, leafy layer high up in the forest.

Comet a chunk of rock and ice from the edge of the solar system.

Coniferous to do with a type of tree with needles and cones.

Constellation a star pattern in the sky.

Continent one of earth's seven major areas of land.

Coral reef a large underwater structure made up of lots of hard coral joined together.

Coral tiny sea animals with a hard, outer skeleton. Together, their skeletons form reefs.

Crater a big hole in the ground.

Dam an obstacle across a river or stream to slow the water flow.

Deciduous to do with a type of tree that has leaves that drop off each year.

Dusk the time of day when it starts to get dark.

Electricity a type of energy. Machines that plug into sockets or have batteries use electricity.

Emergent layer the very top layer of the forest, where only the tallest trees poke up above the rest.

Energy the power to do things.

Environment the surroundings, including the living things and non-living things found there.

Evaporation changing from a liquid to a gas.

Explorer a person who travels in search of information about lands that are not well known.

Extinct (volcano) no longer active and will probably not erupt again.

Forest floor the lowest layer of a forest.

Fuel a substance, such as gasoline, petrol, or diesel, that is burned to make energy.

Fungi a group of living things that get their food from rotting material or other living things.

Galaxy a huge collection of stars, gases, and dust.

Gas a substance that is not a solid or a liquid. A gas spreads out and has no fixed shape.

Gear a wheel with "teeth" that connects to and turns another wheel.

Glacier a slow-moving mass of ice.

Hibernate to go into a deep, sleep-like state through winter to save energy.

Hunt to search for animals to eat.

Hurricane a very large, swirling, and windy storm.

Invertebrate a member of a group of animals without a skeleton in their bodies.

Lagoon a shallow lake or pool.

Mammal a member of a group of animals that has a backbone, has hair on its body, and feeds its young with milk.

Mate a partner for animals to have babies with.

Microphone a device that picks up sounds and turns them into electrical energy.

Microwave a wave of energy that can pass through food and heat it up.

Milky Way our home galaxy.

Moon a ball of rock that travels around Earth or another planet.

Motor a machine that is used to provide energy to move something.

Nest a place built by an animal for sleeping in and laying eggs.

Network a group of things that are connected, such as a computer network or a cellular phone network.

Orbit the path that an object in space takes around another space object.

Oxygen a natural gas in the air that all living things need to survive.

Planet a huge, round object that travels around a star.

Plankton tiny living things, including plants and animals, that float in fresh water or seawater.

Poison a substance that can kill or seriously harm living things.

Predator an animal that hunts and eats other animals.

Prey an animal that is hunted and eaten by other animals.

Radio wave an invisible wave of energy that can travel through the air and space.

Rain forest a thick, often tropical, forest where there is lots of rain.

Recycling taking used things, such as newspapers or bottles, and turning them into new things.

Reptile a member of a group of animals that usually have scales on their skin and lay eggs.

Rover a space robot that can move across the surface of a planet. It sends information about the planet to scientists.

Source the start of something, such as a river.

Star a giant ball of hot gas. Most stars look small in the sky because they are so far away.

Sun Our closest star, in the middle of the solar system.

Satellite any object that travels around a planet.

Seabed the bottom, or floor, of the ocean.

Shellfish invertebrate sea creatures that have hard outer shells, such as crabs and clams.

Silk a very thin thread made by some insects.

Solar system Our Sun, its eight planets, and their moons.

Tadpole a frog after it has hatched from an egg and before it grows legs.

Technology having to do with scientific inventions for practical use.

Tectonic plate a piece of Earth's crust that can rub against other pieces, causing volcanic eruptions and earthquakes.

Tentacles the long, thin parts of an animal usually used for holding and feeling. Some animals' tentacles can sting.

Tide the flowing of water away from or back onto the land.

Undergrowth the grassy, bushy layer of a forest.

Universe everything around us, including the world, space, and everything in it.

Valve an object that controls the flow of a gas or liquid.

INDEX

A

Africa 95
Agoutis 8
Algae 143
Alligators 16
Anacondas 17
Anemones 128
Anglerfish 155
Antarctica 94, 164–165
Anteaters 11
Ants 10, 30
Apes 38
Arctic 115
Arctic Ocean 95, 127, 160–161
Asia 95
Asteroids 200
Astronauts 205, 206, 207
Atlantic Ocean 118
Atmospheres 184–185, 193
Avalanches 106

B

Badgers 49, 57, 61, 77
Ballpoint pens 226–227
Bats 22, 41, 58, 66
Bears 51, 82–83
Beavers 80–81
Bedouin tribe 112
Bees 75, 122
Beetles 23
Bicycles 210–211
Big Bang Theory, The 172–173
Birds of paradise 34–35
Blackberries 68
Blackbirds 58
Blue whales 156–157
Bottlenose dolphins 150–151
Brazil nut trees 8, 41
Bulldog bats 22
Burrows 16, 63, 76
Butterflies 42–43, 49, 74, 122
Buzzards 86

C

Caimans 16, 20
Camels 113
Camouflage 13, 22
Capybaras 17
Cars 232–233
Caterpillars 57
Ceres (dwarf planet) 199
Chameleons 4, 26, 46
Cities 120–121
Clocks 248–249
Clouds 102–103
Clown fish 137
Coasts 126
Comets 200
Computers 228–229, 230, 231
Constellations 171
Continents 94–95
Coral reefs 116–117, 136–137
Crabs 128
Craters 181, 187

D

Deadbolt locks 218
Deep oceans 154–155
Deer 53, 60, 62, 86
Deserts 112–113
Dishwashers 214–215
Divers 140
Dolphins 19, 150–151, 161
Dragonflies 86
Dugongs 144–145
Dwarf planets 198–199

E

Eagles 37, 44–45, 65, 83, 106
Earth 90–91, 92–93, 171, 174, 177, 178, 184
Earthquakes 98–99
Elephants 13
Equator, The 204
Eris (dwarf planet) 198
Europe 95
Evaporation 101

F

Flying fish 147
Flying squirrels 45
Foxes 61, 67, 76
Frogs 7, 23, 24–25, 53, 55
Fungi 54

G

Galaxies 170–171
Galileo 203
Ganymede 191
Giant centipedes 8
Giant squid 162–163
Goblin sharks 154
Golden eagles 65
Gorillas 14–15
Great Barrier Reef 136
Great Bear, The (constellation) 171
Great Red Spot, The 190

H

Hail 105
Hair dryers 244–245
Hammerhead sharks 134
Harpy eagles 44–45
Haumea 199
Hawks 50
Helicopters 224–225
Hook-and-loop fasteners 212–213
Hot-air balloons 242–243
Hoverflies 68
Howler monkeys 32–33
Hubble Space Telescope 202
Huli tribe 111
Hummingbirds 31
Hurricanes 104

I

Iguanas 44
Indian Ocean 95, 127, 144
International Space Station 90, 206–207
Internet, The 230–231
Inuit people 115

J

Jaguars 6, 7, 20–21
James Webb Telescope 203
Jellyfish 148, 158–159
Jupiter 175, 176, 190–191

K

Kapok trees 41
Keck 1 and 2 203
Kepler (space telescope) 205
Keys 218–219
Killer whales 161
Krill 157

L

Lightning 104
Limpets 129
Lizards 26, 27, 44, 84

M

Makemake (dwarf planet) 199
Manatees 18–19
Manta rays 152
Mars 175, 177, 188–189
Mercury 174, 177, 180–181
Meteorologist 103
Meteors 201
Mice 29
Microphones 220
Microwaves 234
Milky Way, The 170
Miranda 195
Monkeys 7, 13, 30, 31, 32, 33, 40, 41, 44
Moon, the 177, 186–187
Moths 27, 36, 66
Mountain lions 107
Mountains 106–107, 189

N

Narwhals 160
Neptune 175, 177, 196–197
Nests 7, 14, 38, 58, 59, 73, 74

North America 94
North Pole 114–115
North Star 171

O

Oceania 95
Oceans 94–95, 101, 116–117, 126–127
Ocelots 9
Octopuses 140–141
Olympus Mons 189
Online games 230–231
Orangutans 38–39
Orcas 161
Otters 78, 130–131
Owls 58, 67

P

Pacific Ocean 94, 127, 144, 154
Parrots 7, 40
Pedals (bicycle) 211
Pelicans 132–133
Penguins 164–165
Pheasants 60
Phones 220–221
Pianos 236–237
Pilots 224, 243
Piranhas 17
Plankton 153
Pluto 175, 177, 198
Porcupine fish 138
Praying mantids 22
Pygmy seahorses 142

R

Rabbits 53, 57, 65, 76
Radio waves 221
Rain 100, 102, 108, 110
Rain forests 5–45, 110–111
Rays 152–153
Recycling 117, 121
Refrigerators 246–247
Rivers 108–109
Robins 53
Rock pools 119, 128–129
Rockets 185, 204, 216–217
Rovers (spacecraft) 189

S

Sailfish 146–147
Salamanders 22
Salmon 82

Satellites 90, 186, 216
Saturn 175, 176, 192–193
Scarlet macaws 40
Sea arches 119
Sea slugs 137
Sea snakes 137, 141
Seagulls 109
Seahorses 142–143
Seals 160
Seashores 118 see also Coasts
Seaweed 129, 131
Sharks 134–135
Shoes 212–213
Sloths 36–37, 44
Slowworms 85
Slugs 66
Snails 66
Snakes 9, 17, 28–29, 31, 49, 55, 84–85, 137
Snow 100, 101, 106, 108, 114–115
Solar system, The 174–175, 176
South America 94
South Pole 114–115
Southern Ocean 126
Space 167–207
Space Launch System 204
Space Shuttle, The 205
Spacecraft see also rockets 216–217
Sperm whales 162
Spiders 9, 75
Squirrels 45, 59, 70
Star maps 171
Starfish 128
Starlings 69
Stars 168–169, 170, 171
Storms 104, 190
Sun 90, 169, 174, 177, 168–179

T

Tadpoles 24
Talons 65
Tapirs 7
Tectonic plates 106
Telescopes 168, 195, 202–203
Termites 6
Tides 118, 126
Tiger sharks 135
Tigers 12–13
Titan (moon) 193
Toads 9, 72
Toilets 238–239
Tokyo 121
Tornadoes 105
Toucans 30
Towns 120–121

Tracks (animal) 60–61
Trains 240–241
Triton (moon) 197
Tuna 146
Turtles 16, 148–149

U

Universe, The 172–173
Uranus 175, 177, 194–195

V

Vacuum cleaners 222
Venom 85, 141, 159
Venus 174, 177, 182–183
Viperfish 154
Volcanoes 96, 106
Voyager spacecraft 205

W

Walruses 160, 161
Wasps 68, 74
Water cycle 100–101
Weasels 53
Weather 102–103
Websites 232
Whales 156–157
Wild boar 56
Wild pigs 8
Wild ponies 71
Wildflowers 53
Wireless connections 231
Wolves 51, 64, 65
Woodpeckers 49, 67
Worms 49, 54, 57, 58, 66

ANSWERS

Jungle Animals Answers

1 False—orangutans are orange and do not have tails. 2 True. 3 False—a group of monkeys is called a troop. 4 False—jaguars sleep in trees. 5 True. 6 True. 7 False—tapirs cannot climb. 8 False—some snakes can swim.

Ocean Animals Answers

1 True. 2 True. 3 False—tiger sharks are about the size of a car. 4 True. 5 True. 6 False—jellyfish are invertebrates. 7 False—porcupine fish blow themselves up like a balloon. 8 False—seahorses eat almost all the time.

Woodland Animals Answers

1 False—conifer forests are green all year round. 2 False—they live in homes called lodges. 3 True. 4 True. 5 True. 6 False—owls mostly hunt at night. 7 True. 8 False—toads like to live in wet areas.

Space Answers

1 True. 2 False—Mercury is the closest planet to the Sun. 3 False—astronauts have only visited the Moon, so far. 4 True. 5 False—there are eight planets circling our Sun. 6 True. 7 True. 8 False—Saturn has lots of moons.

Our World Answers

1 False—deserts can be cold. 2 True. 3 False—it is very hot in Earth's inner core. 4 False—they cover more than half of the planet. 5 True. 6 False—a volcano that is extinct probably won't ever erupt again. 7 True. 8 False—they are formed over many millions of years.

How Things Work Answers

1 False—bicycle pedals are connected to a gear. 2 True. 3 True. 4 True. 5 False—hair dryers need electricity to work. 6 False—helicopters can also fly backward and sideways. 7 True. 8 False—trains have wheels to keep them on the tracks.